ON REDEMPTION FOR ZIMBABWE MY COUNTRY

On Redemption For Zimbabwe My Country

MUSAFARE MUPANDUKI, PhD

To order additional copies of this book, contact:
Xlibris
844-714-8691
www.Xlibris.com
Orders@Xlibris.com
827028

Contents

Preface

Zimbabwe is a country where much seems to happen but nothing seems to change for the betterment of the majority of Zimbabweans

African resistance to colonial domination from 1893 – 1897 posed a massive challenge to the ability of a tiny handful of white settlers to survive in the interior of Africa. To some extent the Shona and Ndebele peoples of Zimbabwe had some grievances but to organize a sustained resistance against the white settlers, as observed by T. Ranger, was an exceptional achievement. In fact resistance expanded from that of the African soldiers alone to that of the entire society. However at best, the resistance produced no improvements for the majority Africans.

The decision by the white settlers in 1923 to opt for responsible government, set colonial Zimbabwe on a unique constitutional course which had much to do with its later ability to defy both Britain and the internal African challenges. The colonial government since 1923 had virtually complete autonomy and successfully used this authority to defend, protect and sustain white settlers privileged position. The Land Apportionment act, The Industrial Conciliatory Act and The Native Affairs Act became the cornerstones of thorough and systematic white domination over land, employment and administration much to the detriment of the African majority.

Although the system was severely challenged by African Nationalist Movements and forced to adjust its methods of control and administration to take into account population growth and demographic changes (particularly the urbanization of both racial groups) its fundamental character remained unaltered much to the detriment of the majority Africans.

The move to federation in 1953, the settlers' demands for the dominion status in 1960, the subsequent negotiations of the 1961 constitution were all designed not to change anything in favor of the majority Africans but to promote and maintain white political and economic power.

The settlers' audacious seizure of independence in 1965 and its ability to stick to it despite great international pressure only confirmed the settlers' ability to do the unexpected and white survival amid the suffering of the black majority.

The 1972 Pearce Commission Settlement was British conspiracy to further the political, economic and social supremacy of the white establishment in Zimbabwe. This was rejected by the Africans when put to a referendum.

The short-lived Zimbabwe-Rhodesia regime did nothing to address the question of changing the colonial state of affairs which among other things included access to the political system over the distribution of the economic goods (land, job opportunities and the African involvement in the creation of their own wealth) and over the system of administration and control.

The Lancaster House Constitution reflected the protection of white interest at the expense of the black majority population. The British made sure that the constitution to usher Zimbabwe to majority rule had plenty of important clauses that were intended to protect the interest of the minority whites.

The Economic Structural Adjustment Program (ESAP) was a reflection of the Ideological Bankruptcy on the part of the leadership in Zimbabwe. Poverty has been on the increase in Zimbabwe, particularly since the implementation of the structural adjustment program (ESAP) in 1991 leading people to blame the reforms for increased poverty. It has been difficult to pinpoint those policies, which have had an adverse effect on poverty and income distribution. This is because a wide range of policies, ranging from trade, to exchange rate to monetary to fiscal and other social policies have been implemented, often at the same time.

Chapter 1

The Road to Independence

The scope of this analysis briefly examines various political and economic interactions from the arrival of white Zimbabweans (herein called white settlers) until the attainment of independence which ushered in another form of colonial government- this time in the form of "black masks". The major focus however will be from the beginning of African resistance movements to present day Zimbabwe.

White settlers entered Zimbabwe in 1890. By the end of the decade (following substantial African resistance) the settlers had succeeded in subduing Africans (Black Zimbabweans) the indigenous proprietors of the country. From that time until April 1980 a small white minority (never more than 5 % of the population) dominated the political and economic life of the country and regimented the black majority to serve its economic needs and confirm its social prejudices. The major components of the social system constructed by this tiny white minority group included the apportionment of the land between black and white- the two racial groups, the development of an industrial color-bar that defined jobs, wages and employment opportunities by race, and the implementation of almost total segregation of races. Through a variety of thinly disguised ruses, access to the political system was foreclosed to all but a handful of Africans.

The white settlers were able to construct this system for two reasons: they possessed the technological and organizational skills necessary to conquer and then directly administer the far larger black majority population and their nominal political and constitutional mentor - the British government allowed them internal autonomy and made no effort to inhibit the growth of a segregated society. This was true both under the British South Africa Company which administered Zimbabwe from 1890 – 1923 and Zimbabwe's unique responsible government constitution after 1923.

Few challenges were posed to this system until world war 2. Policies differed from those practiced elsewhere in Africa both to the north and to the south of Zimbabwe and the whites contemplated the future with equanimity and with little thoughts that the "Rhodesian Way of Life" would ever change. As we shall see later in this analysis, that way of life was never altered by majority rule in 1980. As possessors of advanced technology and bearers of racial and cultural attitudes prevalent in the West, the settlers had little reason to doubt either the moral premises of their society or their indefinite right to perpetuate that same society. Belief in cultural superiority (identical with race) and national progress (identified with white class privilege) dovetailed nicely to reinforce the white community's determination to preserve the society it had organized.

Until April 1980, Zimbabwe's political life had been dominated by the challenge posed to settler rule by the emergence of an indigenous African Nationalist movement calling for independence on the basis of majority rule and by the white settler demands for independence from Britain, independence under white minority government. One called for a complete restructuring of the Zimbabwean politics, the other looked towards establishing conditions that would guarantee the permanence of the system constructed after 1890.

At this point, I will briefly analyze the social, political and economic developments that gave rise to these demands, their articulation both internally and externally, the conflict that arose from these demands, the nature of their resolution and how they have affected political and economic power in contemporary Zimbabwe.

Four different political and economic interactions will briefly dominate this analysis. The first is between white and black in Zimbabwe and concerns the distribution of power within colonial Zimbabwe. African liberation struggle posed a substantial threat to the maintenance of white supremacy. The white settlers responded to these pressures by adding vast new security, legislation from the pre-World War 2 period.

The second interaction was between the local white government and the British government over the limits of white authority within colonial Zimbabwe. A persistent issue of Zimbabwean white politics was the demand for their ever increasing white autonomy. The formation of the Central African Federation in the early 1950's and the 1961 Constitution were important stages in the withdrawal of British control from Zimbabwe. When Britain finally refused to give way fully to white settlers' demands in 1965 the settlers' government seized independence in defiance of Britain and the world. Britain was never prepared to take the steps necessary to challenge this system in any meaningful way.

The third interaction was within the white community itself. In the course of colonial Zimbabwe political history, there was considerable conflict over the best strategies and tactics to ensure continued white political domination and thus economic and social privilege. This conflict took place within a "democratic" political process restricted to the white oligarchy united on the fundamental issue of maintaining the system. The heated white political controversy sometimes seen in colonial Zimbabwe should not prevent us from observing the fundamental reality, namely that white conflict concerned what strategies or priorities to follow in the preservation of the white system. Political conflict in this setting was therefore not synonymous with the offering of real meaningful choice.

The fourth consideration is between black, and white and black in independent Zimbabwe after Lancaster House Constitution. It is hardly a prospect likely to rejoice the heart of any right-thinking Zimbabwean fired with hope of the promised land but discovering instead that the privileged position of the white settler remained very much intact- this time enlarged with the addition of the new black ruling and intellectual elite classes, while the mutilated veterans, heroes of the pre 1980 liberation war, hanging around the streets importuning white pedestrians for an odd cent remained languishing in the rural communities. This will be analyzed in full in the next chapter.

The Emergence of African Nationalism

African nationalism came very late to Zimbabwe. The first was nationwide based party – the African national congress was formed in 1957. By that time Ghana had become independent, Mau Mau in Kenya was nearly over and nationalist movements were already well established in neighboring Zambia and Malawi and South Africa. The nationalist movement in Zimbabwe itself emerged from an indigenous African political tradition that had wavered between resistance and accommodation to the white settlers. Its goals were to redress the social and economic grievances: to achieve this the movement increasingly demanded independence under a majority rule government. To spearhead this movement there were the African-middle class-the petit bourgeoisie, who were only certain of their immediate interests which were not different from those of the white settlers colonial agents. Abolition of the most naked abuses of the colonial government, state-inequality of remuneration of equally trained black and white technicians, forced labor, disenfranchisement and racial discrimination in social intercourse. This, for the African middle class constituted the most urgent task of the independent movement in Zimbabwe.

Zimbabwe African nationalists faced organizational problems which were common elsewhere in Africa, including those of ethnic conflict, of linking rural and urban discontent, and of overcoming the political indifference of non-indigenous migrant workers. These difficulties however paled under the overriding factor of white settler resistance and repression. Like nationalist movements throughout the continent the Zimbabwean Africans engaged in rural and urban protests via meetings, rallies and strikes. They also engaged in international lobbying. In all these activities they made one critical error. They presumed their struggle to be similar to that waged in other British colonies. In Zimbabwe however the colonialist lived side by side with the colonized. Thus the white settlers controlled the political system and this control was accepted by Britain. The British government was unwilling to intervene as the settler government passed the laws and took the steps necessary to destroy the nationalist movement. All that the settlers would concede to the African people was the right to participate nominally within political structures they utterly dominated.

From the end of the 1896-1897 rebellions until world war 2, African political activity was largely limited to a tiny elite who made intermittent efforts to achieve modest improvements in African living conditions. But following the war Africans gradually turned to political protest to draw attention to their grievances. There was much uncertainty about how to proceed and the African pattern continued to swing back and forth between active protest and hope for racial compromise within the colonial setup. For a brief period in the 1960's a few Africans looked to multiracial organizations for solutions to their problems. As history records, Zimbabwe did not prove a fertile ground for trade union organization to flourish. The settler government declined to acknowledge their legitimacy and used force to make the point. Then the white liberals moved in, suffocating the embrace of multiracialism whatever vitality trade unionism had. Thus by the early 1950's, the quasi-political multiracial society had become the fad. Hardwicke Holderness, Eileen Hadolon, Nathan Shamuyarira and the other intellectuals and would-be intellectuals launched the international association in 1953. They debated, had coffee and occasionally danced. In 1955 colonel David Stirling brought his Capricorn Africa society from East Africa to Zimbabwe. This was another inter-racial society on a much bigger scale. Many of the many leaders who were to shape our politics till today were in the ranks of those multiracial societies. The late Leopold Takawira and The James Chikerema were among them.

Meanwhile settler politics also went multiracial. In fact some Africans almost reached the top in Godfrey Huggins' United Federal Party – notably Joshua Nkomo, Jasper Savanhu, Mike Hove, Charles Mzingeli and Chad Chipunza. Stanlake Samkange took an active role in Garfield Todd's Central African Party and Ndabaningi Sithole patched up a long standing disagreement with Todd to join the CAP. All these organizations attempted to build a social and political interaction across racial lines. The problem with these organizations was not that they lacked either motivation or high purpose, but that they were powerless and were not meant to meet the desires and aspirations of the black population in Zimbabwe. Thus they attracted (and this is very important) a tiny group of generally wealthy urban liberals. They were able to make contacts with those few Africans who were well-educated. Each group tended to accept and positively the idea of partnership but none was in a position to give it substance except in an extremely narrow and personal level. It was no wonder that eventually the groups collapsed, the Africans joined nationalist parties and began their migration to prison, those white settlers who retained their liberation began their migration into exile. Multiracialism never had a chance in Zimbabwe so long as the whites firmly retained political power and did not believe they would have to give it up or share it. Each new repressive action drove this point home. Eventually Africans drew the obvious conclusion that they had no choice but to organize their people first, and conditions in both urban and rural areas helped give rise to new African political organization and activity·

On September 12,1957 the new African national congress was born with Nkomo as its leader. A new ANC leadership went into the country and remained there organizing resistance to the white administration, and continued the labor style meetings around the urban areas. Although the urban rallies were drawing good crowds by the end of 1958, they did not concern the white government as much as the political threat seen in the rural organization being created. It was the spread of the resistance movement among the villagers that prompted the government in the early hours of the morning of February 29, 1959 to ban the ANC, and loaded every nationalist leader from village chairman to the top ranks of the party into army trucks. Most of the arrests were in rural branches. Under fresh legislation the ANC leaders were detained without trial in camps all over the country. The only one who escaped was the late Joshua Nkomo who was attending a meeting abroad when the party was banned. While politicking went on in the detention camps, the movement did not have an underground network capable of continuing the work of organizing the people. Unlike Malawi where a similar ban in 1959 sparked a sustained rural resistance which led to the early triumph of the Malawi Congress Party, the Zimbabwean organization was centrally powered. When the power was removed, everything also collapsed. Debate dragged on for almost a year about how to resuscitate the movement. One school of thought believed that it should be re-established as an underground movement, while the other favored the creation of a new party along the lines of the old one. Thus the National Democratic Party(NDP) became ever more deeply involved in a political poker game whose rules were made in London and Harare. It put forward a formal demand for "one man one vote". It organized mass meetings where the law permitted, and sought opportunities to put its case before the white and black publics in a "dignified" manner. The time was auspicious, for 1960 was the year in which all Africa felt the full force of the British foreign secretary Macmillan's "wind of change". The settler government sniffing this "wind of change" decided to change their tactics.

The arrest in July 1960 of Michael Mawema and other NDP leaders precipitated disturbances which ended in what seemed to be a major concession from the then Prime Minister Edgar Whitehead. He called for a constitutional review conference in London. Mawema and his lieutenants became heroes and politics suddenly became a race for office. The chances of becoming a Member of Parliament and of greater things ahead fired the imagination of even the comfortable educated groups, who up to now had remained interested observers and confident onlookers.

In October 1960, Joshua Nkomo, still abroad, was elected to head the party and to lead the delegation to the constitutional conference scheduled to begin in January 1961. Morton Malianga was elected his deputy, George Silundika his secretary-general, Ndabaningi Sithole treasurer, and Robert Mugabe (the deposed President) publicity secretary. A wave of optimism permeated the movement. Outside developments also seemed conclusive to optimistic appraisals. Both in Malawi and Zambia the nationalists seemed close to power after the Monckton Report made clear that federation was in trouble. Many clambered abroad the NDP bandwagon. Could Zimbabwe be far behind ? Many began to worry about how cabinet positions would be allocated. Indeed the nationalists were making the critical error of mistaking foreign developments, tough talk and urban unrest for solid organizing a coherent political strategy where grave errors were to become obvious all too soon.

The 1961 constitution conference held in Harare during January and February, was the critical moment for the Zimbabwean nationalists. Their admission as full participants was a dramatic victory for the NDP, which had regularly called for constitutional change. It seemed that the late Joshua Nkomo's endless travels to the United Nations, London and Third World countries conferences demanding One Man One Vote, were about to pay dividends. The fact that Britain had called for a constitutional conference convinced Nkomo that the NDP could attain political advance through constitutional channels, just as in other British colonial territories.

Joshua Nkomo led the Zimbabwean delegation to the conference. He was joined by the late Ndabaningi Sithole, Chitepo and Silundika. The performance at the conference was woefully inept. They jettisoned the NDP's previous strong position in favor of retaining the reserved clauses and agreed to their removal in exchange for the constitutional council, the declaration of rights and the 15 seats – none of which began to threaten white control of parliament or the repressive machinery of the white settler government in Zimbabwe. The withdrawal of the reserve clauses and the implicit sanctioning of extant discriminating legislation all but generated in the nationalists a permanently ineffective role in the country's politics. They apparently accepted these proposals because they anticipated having white allies in the new parliament, because they came to trust British foreign secretary Duncan Sandys (who chaired the meeting) in the course of the meeting and because they feared that the NDP supporters would accuse them of failure if they rejected every proposal. In the pressure of the conference situation, they made the error of assuming that any agreement would assist their cause and lead towards black rule. This was the pattern in other African countries. But Zimbabwe was different and the nationalists were not cautious enough to understand fully the implications of the pact so eagerly sought by Whitehead and the British government. They also were sadly out of touch with African opinion and in this way they could not get the counsel they would have needed. It was therefore not surprising that they were out-maneuvered at the bargaining table on every major issue and finally accepted a settlement that was tantamount to a complete sell out of the peoples of Zimbabwe. It was therefore not surprising that immediately after the settlement was announced Nkomo came under heavy criticism. Several members of the NDP executive would simply not go along with the fifteen seats settlement. Leopold Takawira wired from London where he handled the NDP's external affairs: "We totally reject Southern Rhodesian constitutional conference agreement as treacherous to the future of the three million Africans. Agreement diabolical and disastrous. Outside world shocked by the NDP's docile agreement".

This was a fairly accurate analysis of the agreements effect, but the damage had been done. Nkomo quickly disowned the agreement but the nationalist movement had squandered its sole opportunity to achieve meaningful constitutional change. This was a blow to Whitehead who could not win without substantial participation of the NDP. The NDP's position was even worse. Having been effectively channeled away from the route of a resistance movement into British style politics, it was unprepared for any form of protest, more vigorous than a boycott of the December 1962 elections.

The movement at this time had genuine grass roots support. By the middle of 1961 there were over 250 000 paid up members of the party. In fact the story might have had a happy ending if nationalist movement had been contending with the British colonial office instead of a colonial settler regime that had long enjoyed the unique position of a self-governing state. According to the late Davis Mugabe, one of the NDP's nationalists and an intellectual, "We have been conditioned to be good churchmen and encouraged to carry out our politics according to British ground rules, but we are facing an entrenched adversary fervently dedicated to preserving a way of life, not a handful of itinerant British civil servants. The Rhodesian ruling group must never be confused with the authorities that have been faced by nationalist movements in other British territories in Africa". NDP then had a following but it was rudderless. Two conferences of the party held during 1961 produced nothing more than a new settlement to party politics and the existing power structures. Radical elements within the NDP organized acts of sabotage on their own, but these were disclaimed and actively discouraged by the party leadership. It was decided that there would be no unconstitutional politics, whatever that meant. But even then the NDP was banned in December 1961 and all the leaders within the country detained.

The optimism of 1960 vanished. Whereas before the conference the NDP's journal "Democratic Voice" had seen "the tragic figure of jittery Sir Edgar Whitehead heading towards damnation", despair and disorganization quickly followed. Following the ban of the NDP the Zimbabwe African Peoples' Union (ZAPU) was formed but its goals, organization, and activities were indistinguishable from the NDP's. It was expected that the movement would go underground and plan for more militant resistance against the white settlers. Nine months later ZAPU was banned before any conference or election had been held. For those nine months, ZAPU followed the footsteps of its predecessor. It gathered thousands upon thousands of faithful supporters who turned up at every meeting. It collected thousands of donations in pounds and subscriptions. The leadership intoxicated by the members who responded confidently proclaimed that "freedom is around the corner", though in retrospect it was never quite clear precisely how the plan was going to fall onto the laps of the nationalist leadership. They talked all day and all night about what would come to pass when the elections are over in December 1962 and negotiations towards majority rule could get under way again. It was indeed an exhilarating time, but the nationalists did not really undertake to develop the power of the wars following the ban of ZAPU was announced in September 1962. Whitehead hoped that this action would win him wavering white votes in the coming election but the effect was the reverse. The rightist Rhodesian Front (RF), led by Winston Field won the election and came to power in December 1962. In a clear tactical move, Field immediately released the 1959 detainees still restricted in the remote desert of Gokwe in the Zambezi valley. All other detainees were released within the next three months. This brought everyone on stage for a power struggle. Chikerema and Nyandoro assumed that they would return to their old positions, if not to even higher echelons as due heroes who had suffered imprisonment for the so called cause. This mentality has remained the hallmark of the former nationalists 'attitude and sadly enough of the young men and women who waged the liberation war heavily supported by the Civilian Zimbabweans – up to present day Zimbabwe.

The new reform group had lost its leverage, and Sithole, Chitepo, Takawira and others found themselves on the fringes. With so many aspirants to secondary positions of power, the party president was in a strong position to dictate terms. Before many months had passed, however, controversial decisions were taken which led nearly all ZAPU's leaders out of the country, and into exile. In fact under a lot of criticism over the leadership's failure to get down to business and to endorse some "ACTS OF SABOTAGE" that had been carried without party authorization, the leadership then issued explicit instructions that all extra-legal activities should cease pending the launch of a "Master Plan" in 1963. As a matter of fact, the master plan was that, while in restriction for three months, Nkomo apparently became convinced that the government would soon seize independence and, therefore thought that the nationalist could best take advantage of this event if they were outside the country when it occurred, prepared to establish a government in exile that could compete with the white regime for international recognition. There was considerable opposition to this suggestion within the former ZAPU executive, but Nkomo persuaded the leaders that this strategy was approved by Julius Nyerere of Tanganyika and other high ranking African leaders.

The departure of the executive to Dar-Eslam in early 1963 stirred widespread resentment in Zimbabwe. In Dar, many ZAPU leaders were shocked when Nyerere strongly rebuked them for leaving Zimbabwe. Talks at the May 1963 inaugural conference in Addis Ababa of the Organization Of African Unity revealed to Sithole and others the grave reservations many African leaders had about Nkomo. Until this point Nkomo's foreign experience had generally been deemed an asset and had given him an aura of expertise and experience that was hard to challenge. Now the doubting Thomas's in the ZAPU executive had hard evidence to support their opposition to Nkomo's external strategies.

Immediately after the Addis Ababa conference the executive returned to Dar where a serious power struggle ensued. Most of the officials now committed themselves to go back to Zimbabwe. Before returning however, they wanted to decide about leadership, whether or not to start a new party, and the nature of future action within Zimbabwe. At this point, Nkomo made a shrewd move that ever after made the "dissidents" position very difficult. Rather than face them in Dar, he returned to Harare where he precipitated the split by denouncing the key nationalists as enemies to the movement. This blunt and direct attack threw those opposing Nkomo (both inside and outside the country) off balance. Most of the executive in Dar faced immediate imprisonment in Zimbabwe because they had jumped bail to leave, and Nkomo being in the country was able to make use the argument that had been most effective used against him – that those outside the country were not interested in struggling for the people.

A sad, wasteful and useless struggle began. The executive returned from Dar and established the Zimbabwe African National Union under the Reverend Ndabaningi Sithole leadership, Nkomo reconstituted ZAPU as People's Caretaker Council (PCC). The formation of open parties in itself was an admission of failure, for many leaders, particularly in ZANU favored a militant underground campaign directed against the white regime.

There is no way to gauge accurately which party had the greatest support, although PCC was stronger. Neither party followed the single course that was most likely to lead to popular approval and internal ascendancy- that is, relentless struggle against the white regime. This was to come much later. The split was not based on ethnic or tribal lines, although most Ndebele's stood by Nkomo. Of the fifteen of the seventeen past numbers of the ANC, NDP and ZANU executive that can be counted for, eight stayed with Nkomo and seven went with Sithole. Like their white counterparties the crux of the split was not even political, except as they differed over past actions (or the lack thereof). Both parties exposed similar goals: independence under majority rule, relentless opposition to colonialism and imperialism and commitment to African socialism and Pan-Africanism both of which they had no clear understanding, in how they would work in an independent Zimbabwe.

In the year before both parties were banned they engaged in dismal internecine warfare. Little attention was paid to the putative enemy – the white regime settlers were free to pick off the nationalists as they pleased. Nkomo was restricted in April 1964, Sithole went to prison in May 1964. The same could be said of many other nationalists. For the PCC, ZANU did not exist, for ZANU no nationalist movement was possible if led by Nkomo. Behind these intractable positions the Africans stood divided against the white government from 1963 until when ZANU and ZAPU were forced by the OAU Liberation Committee to form a joint military command of the liberation movement in 1975.

Between 1959 and 1964 five major nationalist organizations were banned in Zimbabwe. Could this have been avoided? or was it inevitable or even necessary? For my part the deeper I enter into the political circles of the Zimbabwe nationalist movements then and the nationalist political leadership today, the surer I become that the greatest single danger that threatened them then and continues to be hazardous today is the lack of clear direction and an ideology that is deeply rooted in the Zimbabwe way of life – an ideology that takes into account the rich Zimbabwean cultures. The late Davis Mugabe, a very close friend of mine and a Zimbabwean nationalist himself argued that the Zimbabwean nationalist movement failed as an "effective revolutionary force because it moved from one European model to another without even sinking its roots deep into the

African soil". It was indeed an unfortunate experiment in trying to defeat the enemy through the rules of his own game. Indeed these observations are difficult lessons learned from negotiating experiences with Britain and from organizational experiences within Zimbabwe. This will be analyzed in the chapter dealing with the future.

In stressing primarily urban organization and constitutional political advance, the nationalist explicitly accepted the possibility of internal suppression but expected that, in turn, Britain would eventually come to their rescue. As a result (and until very late) the nationalist never formulated a revolutionary perspective with which to confront the setter government. They interpreted the Zimbabwean struggle as analogous to those waged in Malawi and Zambia, and other British colonies. The nationalists were wrong. The settler regime (as they were to discover later) was determined to resist nationalist pressure and often nationalist organizations played right into white settler regime hands. The nationalists also fundamentally misunderstood the nature and pattern of British/white settlers' relations, and grossly overestimated Britain's commitment to Zimbabwean Africans.

Indeed it became quite clear that it was impossible to achieve the nationalists' aspirations through the British and international help without resort to confrontation. As we have seen in this analysis, three nationalist parties which were necessarily founded to operate within the prevailing political system were banned and their organization destroyed. In these circumstances, and in the absence of British intervention, a peaceful transition to African majority rule was never a real possibility under a constitutional system that could be made to impede African advance and to ensure white settler domination. The result was that, the Africans deprived of any constitutional means of opposing the white minority regime, or of any British support in doing so, chose the path of direct confrontation.

CHAPTER 2

The Unilateral Declaration for Independence and the Liberation Struggle

The author looks at the struggle to maintain white supremacy in what is now Zimbabwe, a hundred years after Cecil Rhodes' pioneers carved out a British colony there.

Ian Smith

In September 1890 Cecil Rhodes' pioneer column trundled into Mashonaland to establish Fort Salisbury and the new colonial state named after its founder: Rhodesia. 90 years later white-ruled Rhodesia became the independent state of Zimbabwe. In the 1890s the first settlers brutally suppressed a series of 'native rebellions' or *Chimurenga* (the Shona word for 'resistance'), as the indigenous peoples called their defense against alien invaders. Thereafter, white Rhodesians fought a number of wars on behalf of the British Empire and then indulged in a traumatic civil war that lasted fourteen years and took over 30,000 lives. The bitterness remains, not least among the many – often partisan – writers who are struggling to explain and explore the war's many facets, some still shrouded in secrecy.

The very nature of the act of rebellion against the Crown – UDI, the unilateral or, to its critics, the illegal, declaration of independence in 1965 – is still fiercely debated. For the white Rhodesians, it was, in retrospect, a colossal blunder. The self-governing British colony of Southern Rhodesia, to use its correct designation, was practically independent in all but name. That had been the case since 1923 or, arguably, 1911. Provided the right kind of constitutional verbiage could have been conjured up, both Labor and Conservative administrations in London would have been happy to remove that colonial albatross from its neck. If Ian Smith, the Rhodesian prime minister, had been half as cynical as some of the British politicians he dealt with, he could have agreed to any legal wording, secured Rhodesian independence and then tore up the agreement. But his Rhodesian Front Party wanted more than a legalization of the status quo; it was committed to achieving full sovereignty so as to turn the clock back.

The white supremacists wanted to strip the African majority of the few rights it held in 1965. Many white Rhodesians felt that they had an unquestionable right to the same measure of independence as the other states in the former Central African federation, Zambia (Northern Rhodesia) and Malawi (Nyasaland). The whites in power in Salisbury argued that they had proved their experience and success in governing the country, especially compared with the untried black politicians who took over in the neighboring states. Smith and his followers reckoned that London would not, in the final analysis, use force against the rebel colony, partly because of its brave war record on behalf of Britain: per head of (white) population Rhodesia had contributed more in both world wars than any other part of the empire, including the United Kingdom. More especially, a large proportion of the white Rhodesian population had served in the British armed forces in the Second World War, and close ties existed with the senior echelons of the British services. Many British ex-servicemen, especially from the Royal Air Force, had settled in the prosperous colony.

Whatever the moral and political arguments, Britain did not use force to crush the rebellion. There is little doubt now that after a few resignations here and there, the army, the Royal Navy and even the Royal Air Force (supposedly the most disaffected service) would have carried out any orders to subdue the first national treason against the Crown since the American War of Independence. On the Rhodesian side, UDI was a military bluff. According to a very senior Rhodesian intelligence officer, 'except for one or two senior members of the British South Africa Police [the Rhodesian police force] and a few South African hotheads in the depleted Rhodesian Light Infantry', white Rhodesians would not have resisted a rapid show of force. The bluff, though, was never called. That master tactician, the British Prime Minister Harold Wilson, threw away his best cards by renouncing force at the outset. He opted for sanctions instead. Threatening 'to throw the book' at the Rhodesian Front, he simply flicked a few pages... one at a time. Sanctions were a gesture, never a concerted policy. Until 1974 they boosted rather than undermined the rebel colony.

Sanctions failed to end the war in 'weeks rather than months', as Wilson had promised, for a number of reasons. Above all, they were applied slowly, half-heartedly and cynically. Britain, for one, kept on supplying oil to the rebels. Washington made a point of trading in strategic materials, especially chrome. The Soviet bloc accounted for more than half of Rhodesia's illicit deals, as Ken Flower, the head of Rhodesia's Central Intelligence Organization (CIO), made clear in his recent memoirs. Many of these transactions were arranged through pliant companies in Austria, West Germany, Switzerland and Belgium. Heavy machinery came from the East, usually in shipments brought by Yugoslavs who had no qualms about flying to Salisbury, as long as their passports were not stamped. As one Rhodesian Special Branch officer involved with these deals noted recently: 'Slavs were popular with [Rhodesian] immigration officers because they inevitably 'brought gifts of plum brandy and offered around cigarettes of heavily scented tobacco'.

The most important sanctions-breakers, however, were the South Africans. This led to the greatest paradox of the Rhodesian war. Rhodesia broke away from Britain to avoid black rule and then, with the onset of the guerrilla war, became completely dependent upon a South African regime which was even more determined than Britain to establish a black leader in Salisbury. Above all, the South African government dreaded the possibility of a victorious Marxist army marching through the streets of Salisbury, a precedent which it feared might be repeated in Pretoria. Rhodesia transformed itself from a self-governing British colony into an occasionally truculent, but inevitably subservient, sector of Afrikaner imperium. Ian Smith became, in effect, the leader of another South African homeland. Pretoria selfishly manipulated its Rhodesian satrapy ('while making a huge profit on sanctions-breaking to the captive rebel market) by providing just enough military support to allow Smith time to reach the elusive 'settlement' with black 'moderates'. This policy totally backfired and merely served to lengthen the savage war.

Until 1973 Britain tried hard to settle with Salisbury. In each settlement proposal London offered more concessions. Wilson was torn by what he termed his four 'constituencies': the Conservatives, the Commonwealth, the United Nations and South Africa. The inevitable compromises that ensued gave Wilson's policies 'that madcap flair', in the words of the American ambassador to Zambia. The end result was an impasse: no force, no confrontation with South Africa and no 'sell-out'. The inherent contradictions meant more leaky sanctions and growing white Rhodesian intransigence. Thus ensued the long diplomatic melodrama punctuated by angry encounters on ships, foolish estimates and silly superlatives. These negotiations gave Smith credibility at home and some respectability abroad. Meanwhile, Pretoria played a subtle game until 1978, when the Prime Minister, P.W. Botha, risked nearly all to back the so-called 'internal settlement', with Bishop Muzorewa playing the role of 'useful idiot', to use a Marxist phrase.

In 1965, few of the key players in the Rhodesian saga foresaw the main elements of the unfolding Greek tragedy. Not only was black rule inevitable, but it was almost inevitable that, once they were allowed to get away with UDI, Rhodesian whites were unlikely to accept that fate without a considerable struggle. That struggle was bound to be prolonged, if, firstly, the black nationalist movement was to become divided, and, secondly, international pressures, especially sanctions, were not comprehensively applied. Black nationalists spent as much time fighting each other as combating Smith's troops, and Pretoria made a political point of circumventing sanctions to show that an even larger possible set of sanctions against apartheid would not work. In the 1970s comprehensive sanctions against South Africa as well as Rhodesia were not on the main political agenda.

The War for Independence

Zimbabwean Bush **War**, also known as the Second Chimurenga Struggle, was a war which lasted from July1966 to 1979 and led to universal suffrage, the end of white minority-rule in Rhodesia, and the creation of the Republic of Zimbabwe.

The military reasons for white Rhodesia's long survival were essentially threefold: nationalist divisions, the operational efficiency of the Rhodesian forces and massive South African support, particularly in the last phase of the fighting. The South Africans first intervened in 1967, when they sent approximately 2,000 members of the South African Police (SAP) to help guard the northern border with Zambia. Policemen were sent for two reasons. Salisbury always insisted that it was counteracting a criminal conspiracy by external Communist-inspired agitators, not an internal civil war against racial injustice, and, secondly, Pretoria did not initially contribute army units as this could have been construed as a military intervention in a British colony.

Rhodesia's senior commanders were hostile to this initial intercession, but they were firmly told by Smith that the South Africans were needed for political as much as military reasons. Often ill-trained, overconfident and bored, many of these policemen performed abysmally. Until a number of them were killed by the guerrillas, their operations assumed 'a holiday ramp atmosphere', according to Rhodesian observers. Their reluctant allies used to call the SAP contingents 'clumpiest' because of their poor bush craft. Eventually the Rhodesians were issued with explicit orders not to call their allies by disparaging names. (Presumably an order ignored as much as the official instructions to the Rhodesian Special Air Service to desist from referring to their own Combined Operations HQ as the 'Muppet Show'.)

The South Africans rapidly learnt, however, for they were in Rhodesia to improve their own counter-insurgency skills as much as 'to pull their neighbor's chestnuts out of the fire', as their Prime Minister, John Vorster, put it. Vorster used this force as a political lever. In 1975 he recalled the police (but left his pilots and helicopters on loan), as a part of his *detente* exercise with black nationalist leaders such as Kenneth Kaunda. Then, in 1976, during the American peace initiative led by Henry Kissinger, Vorster played a major role in bringing Smith to heel. Tying Smith down, confessed Vorster, was 'like trying to nail jelly to a wall'. But the Afrikaner did just that when he cut off nearly all military shipments to Smith. Rhodesian troops in the field were sometimes reduced to a few days' supplies of ammunition. In this sense, Vorster did as much as the guerrilla leader Robert Mugabe to break the Rhodesian fighting spirit. Pretoria feared that an escalation of the war would prompt direct Cuban and Russian involvement, just as had happened in the Angolan war.

Rhodesian troops on operations at the Mozambique border; the 1974 revolution in Portugal and subsequent independence for her colonies transformed the strategic situation to the detriment of the Smith regime. Courtesy of the author.

So Smith was compelled to utter the unsayable and accept majority rule (though he never defined the term). White morale slumped. But the ensuing conference in Geneva collapsed and Vorster resumed military aid. More pilots and equipment were loaned, particularly aircraft such as Alouettes and Canberra's which, because they were in both Rhodesian and South African arsenals, could be passed off as Rhodesian weapons. One of the most vital forms of assistance was the loan of army signalers, who formed 'V Troop'. This unit eavesdropped on nearly all the guerrilla and host states' intelligence and military communications. P.W. Botha, as the South African defense minister, had always tried to back Ian Smith to the hilt, but Vorster and particularly his eminence grise, the intelligence chief Hendrik van den Bergh, spiked some of Botha's more adventurous plans to intervene in Rhodesia, as well as in Angola and Mozambique. When Botha became prime minister in September 1978, South African equipment and troops (often in Rhodesian uniform) poured in. Large South African helicopters (the French-supplied Pumas) and the crack Reconnaissance Commandos took part in Rhodesian cross-border raids ('externals' in Rhodesian parlance), especially against guerrilla bases in Mozambique. In raids elsewhere, against Zambia and Angola, South African air force Mirage fighters stood in reserve should Russian- or Cuban-piloted MiG's have intervened. Numerous South African agents also infiltrated Rhodesia, and the local Special Branch was hard-pressed to keep these supposedly allied spies under surveillance. Pretoria also recruited widely to establish an extensive spy network for the time when Zimbabwe became independent.

The stage was now set for a rapid increase in the tempo of the war. The Cubans had indeed prepared a conventional invasion plan for Russia's proteges, Joshua Nkomo's army, based in Zambia. Nkomo's better-trained troops formed, with Mugabe's guerrillas, the Patriotic Front alliance which was dedicated to destroying white minority rule.

By mid-1979, 95 per cent of Rhodesia was under martial law. In effect, the senior generals, led by Lieutenant-General Peter Walls, who had served in the Black Watch, and Ken Flower of the CIO, a Cornishman, were running the country behind the facade of the new prime minister, Bishop Muzorewa. The bishop had emerged victorious from the elections of April 1979, which had been boycotted by the Patriotic Front. Ian Smith, however, was still in the Cabinet, as Minister without Portfolio, or 'Minister with all the Portfolios', as Nkomo dubbed him. Hardliners in the Rhodesian Front still insisted that the war could be won militarily; under Muzorewa the raids on the neighboring states were intensified, but already large swathes of the country could only he entered by the security forces in strength.

There were no formal liberated areas inside Rhodesia, but government infrastructure – schools, clinics, animal dip-tanks and local government – had been wiped out in the more isolated 'native reserves' or Tribal Trust Lands, where most of the approximately six million Africans lived. Guerrilla commissars, especially in eastern Rhodesia, along the long porous border with Mozambique, were building up rudimentary administrative systems to support Mugabe's Zimbabwe African National Union (ZANU) party. The Marxist government in Mozambique fully backed Mugabe and sent in at least 500 Mozambican regular troops to assist ZANU inside Rhodesia. White power was being swamped by the sheer numbers of the guerrillas. As one member of the elite Selous Scouts put it, after a major raid into Mozambique in 1979: 'We knew then that we could never beat them. They had so much equipment and there were so many of them. They would just keep coming with more and more.'

Short of international recognition and the removal of sanctions, Muzorewa's shaky government, controlled and protected as it was by the Rhodesian security forces, could not have survived for perhaps more than another year. Only massive South African military intervention could have propped it up, but that might have prompted the kind of Eastern bloc conventional assault that so concerned Pretoria. The South African government never recognized the Smith or Muzorewa regimes, nor did any other state. The vital factor was always British recognition. Despite the fact that a Conservative observer group officially acknowledged the fairness of the April 1979 election, the new British Prime Minister, Margaret Thatcher, refused to accord diplomatic recognition to Muzorewa's government. That was the bishop's death knell.

And so the Rhodesian saga was to be decided largely on the battlefield. The war can be divided into three stages: from UDI to 1972, the small Rhodesian security forces were engaged in a conflict they could have won decisively in *military* terms; from 1972 to 1976, it could be described as 'no-win' war; and from 1976 to 1980 the Rhodesians were sucked into a war they were manifestly losing. If the Lancaster House talks had not intervened, military defeat was around the corner for white Rhodesia.

CHAPTER 3

The Lancaster House Conference and Constitution

The armed struggle posed an obvious threat to internal security throughout the whole country despite South African assistance against the liberation forces. It was therefore not surprising that from 1975 onwards the freedom fighters had involved the whole of Zimbabwe in such an extended conflict that something had to be done. Undoubtedly the freedom fighters had developed the capability to sustain active military pressure for a consistent length of time to such an extent that hard choices faced the white settlers and their protector- South Africa. Thus the African war of liberation eventually culminated in the Lancaster House Constitutional Conference between Britain, the settlers' and nationalist leaders.

The Lancaster House Conference Participants

British delegation[

Peter Carrington, 6th Baron of Carrington (Chairman)

- Sir Ian Gilmour
- Sir Michael Havers
- David Ormsby-Gore, 5th Baron Harlech

- Richard Luce
- Sir Michael Palliser
- Sir Antony Duff
- D. M. Day
- R. A. C. Byatt
- Robin Renwick, Baron Renwick of Clifton
- P. R. N. Fife
- Sir Nicholas Fenn, Head of News Department of the Foreign Office
- George Walden
- C. D. Powell
- P. J. Barlow
- R. D. Wilkinson
- A. M. Laden
- R. M. J. Lynne
- M. J. Richardson
- C. R. L. de Chas iron
- A. J. Phillips
- M. C. Wood

Patriotic Front delegation[edit]

- Robert Mugabe- ZANUPF leader and future President of Zimbabwe
- Joshua Nkomo- ZAPU leader and future Vice President
- Joseph Msika- ZAPU leader, moderate, detained with Nkomo, future government minister
- Edgar Tekere,- future Government minister, expelled from the party in 1988 after he denounced plans to establish a one-party state in Zimbabwe. He also emerged as a vocal critic of the massacre of civilians in Matabeleland after government launched a crackdown against so-called dissidents in the region. He formed his own party, Zimbabwe Unity Movement (ZUM) in 1989 ahead of general elections in 1990.
- General, Josiah Tongogara, ZANLA general, from ZANU militant external wing
- Earnest Kadungure, ZANU, future Finance secretary

- Dr. Herbert Ushewokunze– first health minister, director of energy and transportation, director of political affairs. Flamboyant and often controversial, he often clashed with the Mugabe administration and was thrown out of the government, welcomed back in, then thrown out again. He died in 1995 and was buried in Zimbabwe's national cemetery. He was declared a national hero.
- Dzingai Mutumbuka– future minister of education
- Josiah Tungamirai, Future Airforce Commander
- Edson Zvobgo, Lawyer, Harvard, future government minister
- Dr Simba Mubako
- Prof Walter Kamba, later Vice-Chancellor of the <u>University of Zimbabwe</u>
- Joseph Msika, ZAPU leader, detained with Nkomo, future vice-President
- George Silundika, ZAPU Publicity Secretary
- Aristotle Chambati, Future Minister of Finance (Died of cancer 6 months after accepting the post)
- L Baron
- S K Sibanda
- E Mlambo
- C Ndlovu
- E Siziba
- K Ndoro

Zimbabwe-Rhodesia delegation

- Prime Minister Bishop Abel Muzorewa
- S C Mundawarara
- E L Bulle
- F. Zindoga
- D C Mukome
- G B Nyandoro
- Reverend Reverend Ndabaningi Sithole
- L Nyemba
- Chief Kayisa Ndiweni
- Z M Bafanah
- Ian Smith
- D C Smith

- R Cronje
- C Andersen
- Dr J Kamusikiri
- G Pincus
- L G Smith
- Air Vice Marshal Herald Hawkins
- Dr E M F Chitate
- David Zamchiya
- Simpson Mutambanengwe
- M A Adam
- P Clay pole
- Gordon Chavunduka

LANCASTER HOUSE AGREEMENT AND THE ZIMBABWE INDEPENDENCE

A Game, Leadership, and Power.

The intent of this chapter is to extend theory and provide tools for analyzing the complexities of the Lancaster House negotiations. Coalition theory, decision theory, game theory, and leadership theory are each applied to the negotiations leading to the independence of Zimbabwe. There is no common and shared definition of what a negotiation is. Zartman(1994) defines negotiation as a "process of combining conflicting positions into a common position under a decision rule of unanimity, a phenomenon in which the outcome is determined by the process"(p.15).

However, most theories of negotiations share the notion of negotiations as a process. Yet, they differ in their description of a process. Structural Analysis considers this process to be a power game. Strategic analysis thinks of it as a repetition game (Game Theory). Integrative Analysis prefers the more intuitive notion of process, in which negotiations undergo successive stages, e.g. pre-negotiation, stalemate, settlement. Especially structural, strategic and processual analysis build on rational actors, who are able to prioritize clear goals, are able to make trade-offs between conflicting values, are consistent in their behavioral pattern, and are able to take uncertainty into account(Watkins et al, 2001, pp. xvii-xxi).

Domestic Parties to the Dispute

Ending a civil war is usually difficult. Organizational inertia, tunnel vision, thinking, and miscommunication all work against early reconciliation and make cooperation difficult. Once fighting begins, plans are set in motion and attitudes toward the enemy become fixed in ways that are not easily reversible (Walter, 1997, p.336). Even if opponents agree to negotiate, they still face the risks and uncertainties of cooperation difficult. Will an opponent fulfill its side of the agreement? Or will the compromise itself turn out an inherently bad deal? Civil wars do not end up with some type of explicit settlement. Current explanations claim that power asymmetries, indivisible stakes, bargaining difficulties, opposing identities make settlement in civil wars nearly impossible.

In Rhodesia, successive white settler colonial leaders, including Ian Smith, repeatedly rejected power-sharing solutions from 1976. The October 1976 All-Party Geneva Conference on Rhodesia mediated by U.S. secretary of state Henry Kissinger and John Vorster failed to achieve the goal of power-sharing. The so-called internal settlement of March 3, 1978, the Rhodesian Front own attempt to come to terms with the black majority without the Patriotic Front of Joshua Nkomo and Robert Mugabe, reached an agreement on granting one person one vote but interests of the white settlers were protected. Thus, it gave the White population 28 of the 100 seats in parliament, a blocking fourth for constitutional change under the new constitution. In addition, control over public service, police and defense forces remained on white hands, preserving the power to undemocratically alter policy outcomes ex post facto.

Habeeb(1998) has developed a power theory that applies to the issue under discussion in this analysis. Based on the conceptual framework, Habeeb develops a theory that presumes that the process and outcome of any asymmetrical negotiation is essentially determined by the dynamic changes in the balance of issue-specific power. Whereas aggregate structural power(which essentially refers to an actor's resources, capabilities, and position vis-à-vis the external world as a whole[p.17]) has a major direct and indirect (through its impact on the tactical power) influence on negotiations, it does not determine the process and outcome of negotiations.

Hence, in the case of Ian Smith, despite all his aggregate power, in October 1979, he compromised, revealing the preferences in a Game Theory T(Temptation) >DC(Democratic Compromise) > CW(Civil War) > S(Sucker) (Prisoner's Dilemma). But Ian Smith himself refused to budge and had to be removed by his own party. This incident has been interpreted in two ways. The first is that he was sincere in his wish to go down fighting rather than compromise, giving Deadlock preferences, again, in a Game Theory T > CW > CR > S (Stedman, 1991). The second is that this was tactical ploy where he counted on being removed, allowing himself to be seen fighting to the bitter end, giving Prisoner's Dilemma preferences (Tamarkin, 1990).

The war in Rhodesia was about majority rule but not necessarily about democracy since an undemocratic Black regime was possible(Nyhamar, 1999, p.6). Both the Zimbabwe African Peoples' Union (ZAPU) led by Joshua Nkomo, and the Zimbabwe African National Union (ZANU) led by Robert Mugabe officially endorsed democracy as a solution to end the war. The split between the two parties in 1963, had occurred over whether Zimbabwean should be their own liberators and therefore adopting a military strategy, and ZANU broke away to begin the armed struggle. In the meantime, in both 1976 and 1978, Nkomo's attempts to negotiate a separate agreement with Smith failed because Smith was not prepared to accept majority rule. It was therefore not surprising that Nkomo adopted the military strategy only when compromise failed, and when military inactivity had become a military liability(ibid, p.7).Interestingly, Nkomo did not opt for guerrilla warfare, but building a conventional force to deliver Salisbury the final blow(Tamarkin, 1990). It was no coincidence that Nkomo's military strategy led to very little actual fighting. Assurance Game players will opt for the military strategy if others choose the military strategy, but Nkomo's first preference remained the CR outcome, yielding the preferences, CR > T > CW > S (Assurance Game)

Robert Mugabe did want majority rule in Zimbabwe, but ideologically he believed that allowing multiparty parties might cause ethnically diverse African communities to fall apart. He never thought that Ian Smith would yield on the crucial issue of majority rule before the military situation was ripe, and considered negotiating with him politically harmful. In any case Smith had vowed that majority rule would come to Rhodesia not in a thousand years. But Mugabe's reluctance did not stem for ideology or principle, as a British diplomat stated, "He believed in armed struggle, because of Smith" (Stedman, 1993, p.138). ZANU was militarily stronger and more active than ZAPU in the armed liberation struggle, suffering large loses---7ooo dead in 1979 alone out of a total of force of 50,000. The morale of ZANLA forces unbroken and Robert Mugabe was on his way to military victory, but he was not ideologically opposed to a settlement (Stedman, 1993). Thus, applying the power theory, Mugabe had alternatives, commitment and control to shape the direction of power balances in the negotiations. His preferences in the Game Theory were thus T > DC > CW > S (Prisoner's Dilemma).

External Parties to the Dispute

I call these secondary parties, the Front-line- states, South Africa, Great Britain, and to a lesser degree the United States of America, Nigeria, Commonwealth and the Organization of African Unity.

The Front-line Presidents had made it clear to the leaders of the Patriotic Front that they wanted peace.

Although remaining on the periphery, the Carter administration did make certain contributions that ultimately led to a successful conference. The conference had stalemated over the question of financing land resettlement and redistribution schemes a majority rule government rule government might undertake. Nkomo and Mugabe balked at the idea of compensating whites for land that the PF felt had been stolen from its original African owners. While Carter's commitment on this issue was rather convoluted and cautious, just offering the possibility of U.S. aid to compensate landowners was enough to offer the PF a face-saving way out of the impasse (Davidow, p.65).

The Importance of The British Mediation

Acting as a bridge between internal decision making and external negotiating and reconciling the divergent interests of fractious constituencies demands leadership grounded in credibility and skill rather than authority. Lord Carrington was the British mediator and he had two sources of power. One was the power emanating from his position as foreign secretary of Great Britain which automatically gave him some amount of authority over the sides. However, the Commonwealth's mandate to Britain (i.e., to Carrington) for a mediation effort was his really power. It was this mandate that gave him a wide-ranging freedom to 'bully' the sides into an agreement whether they wanted it or not. Patriotic Front could denounce Britain but not Commonwealth because many of their patrons and allies were part of it.

Stakes of the Mediator

Lord Carrington had his wounded prestige from his previous mediation effort. Moreover, he had mining interests in Rhodesia, South Africa and Namibia. Britain had its prestige to deal with as well. Authorities in Britain probably felt that this conflict had gone on for too long and they were being humiliated. This feeling of humiliation explains why in this mediation effort they tried to keep it 'in the family' and not include 'strangers' e.g., US. Britain also worried that this problem would affect its relations with the Commonwealth. Prime minister Margaret Thatcher, being more worried about economics, wanted to be rid of this problem. Great Britain had much to lose economically if things continued: its economic relations with sub-Saharan Africa were in jeopardy. Nigeria, Britain's most important trading partner in Sub-Saharan Africa, was threatening British interests. Nigeria was not allowing British companies to tender for contracts. Britain was economically in dire straits at the time. The OPEC crisis was still in the minds of the British people. This was the fourth mediation effort in as many years and the Rhodesians had declared their independence nearly two decades ago. Thousands of people had already died and many had emigrated or had become refugees. Rhodesia's economy was in bad shape but so was the region's economy. Militarily, Rhodesia's position was worsening. Therefore, this mediation effort cannot be called early. All sides seem to have been ready for another mediation attempt either because they were coerced into it or because they saw it as being in their interests.

Leadership

Leadership defined in terms of innovative thinking, inventiveness and problem-solving skills, seems to have been evident throughout the course of negotiations. Lord Carrington obviously played a key leadership role in the negotiations by structuring and shaping the agenda, moving negotiations forward and inventing novel solutions to at first glance seemed to be intractable problems.

Lord Carrington realized that white economic privileges not only made the democratic compromise outcome more attractive, but, importantly offered a credible guarantee of long-term benefits for a group surely facing long-term political marginalization. Thus white economic privileges made the Democratic strategy rational even if the Whites were to become a permanent minority without any say in the iterated political game or if the iterated political game is cut short by the winners of the first elections, making it difficult to generalize this aspect of the Zimbabwe experiences to cases where the parties can only be rewarded by the political game (Nyhamar, p.18). Hence, Carrington's tactics at Lancaster House was to keep issues strictly separated. The first issue was the constitution, then the transitional arrangements, and finally the ceasefire. After six weeks of hard negotiations, ZANU and ZAPU, who had united politically under the PF umbrella for Lancaster House, accepted the constitution on September 18, 1979. Agreement was reached with Lord Carrington fully in control of issues and proposals, in spite of many PF attempts to wrestle the initiative from him (Davidow, 1984, p.61). Moreover, no ultimatum from the Front Line presidents was necessary to make the PF accept the Constitution, even with property rights enshrined in the Constitution: Land had to be voluntarily sold and paid for at once with full, market-level compensation. This provision made land reform impossible, setting aside the most important political issue in Zimbabwe. It is true that one persistent source of tension has always been land segregation. This complex feature of Rhodesian life permeates all questions of economic, social, and political life and no aspect of Rhodesian politics can be understood without finding a solution to the land issue(Bowman, 1973)

Equilibrium Outcomes

Lord Carrington gained control over the agenda by preserving the privilege to present proposals. Moreover, he and his team engaged in a kind of shuttle diplomacy; the actors sat in separate rooms, bargaining with Carrington rather than with each other. This minimized the problem created by the many equilibrium solutions, because all actors were forced to concentrate on this one and same solution. Note should, however be taken that this does not necessarily mean that the parties at Lancaster House had a wide zone of acceptable solutions. Roughly the same amounts of utility may be represented in many concrete ways, giving considerable leeway even with the thinnest of acceptable zones. Davidow (1984:110) argues that "Carrington's tactics enabled him to obtain concessions from each party they would not otherwise have granted, but more importantly, the parties were able to converge on an acceptable outcome in only four months".

Implication for transition to majority government

There was an agreement which resulted in the establishment of the Republic of Zimbabwe. It was mostly an integrative solution. Almost all types of integrative bargaining took place.

Neither of the conflicting parties achieved their initial demands and were faced with unfavorable British options. The options were disliked by both parties. The British believed that the only way forward was for them to formulate the options and then to present it to the conflicting parties (while making it clear that the choices were between accepting it and leaving the table). Bridging was thus used. The Rhodesians had initially demanded recognition and the ending of economic sanctions. They were not granted these but rather received some provisions and safeguards which, when compared to what they had, must have looked weak. Yet the remnants of Colonialism. Instead, they agreed (with pressure from their patrons) to not only give the Rhodesian citizens automatic rights to Zimbabwean citizenship but also to reserve twenty seats in the parliament for the whites.

The reestablishment of British colonial power was another example of bridging. The Rhodesians were not seen as directly turning power over to the PF, and free elections (under British control) could take place; the PF was sure that it would win. Both sides had initially different goals than what they finally agreed to but the final deal that they offered was still acceptable (or forced to be acceptable).

Expanding the pie can be seen in at least three cases. The PF obtained the promise of funds from the U.S. in return for dropping their demands for compensation of land. The PF also received more assembly points for their freedom fighters (a critical issue as the PF knew that their soldiers would be vulnerable to a conventional attack, especially from the Rhodesian air force). British and Commonwealth forces were also stationed in these points which would have meant that an attack on the freedom fighters would also have meant an attack on the British.

It can be argued that the most important case of expanding the pie was when Britain made it clear to the parties that its role would not end at the table but that it would also be involved in implementation of the agreement. I think this factor of bringing a 'policeman' was helpful to the parties who greatly mistrusted one another.

Logrolling can be seen in the issue of peacekeepers. The British knew that the Rhodesians would not accept UN peacekeepers but they also knew that the PF insisted on the presence of peacekeepers. Therefore, the British (with some nominal Commonwealth contribution) took over the role of peacekeeping. It can also be said that there was logrolling on the two most important issues: land and democracy. The PF "had got the main concession of the creation of democracy" and compromised on the land (Charlton: 129).

All of the sides believed that the elections would create a result favorable to them and the British used this belief. This can be considered a form of non-specific compensation because the British held out the bait of elections in return for acceding to the agreement.

The Rhodesians said that the British had given them (secret) assurances that Mugabe would not be allowed to form a government and that instead Nkomo would be part of a coalition government. The Rhodesians maintained that it was this belief that made them lenient (Bayer, 2002). In my opinion, this would be a form of cost-cutting: elections take place but the most militant side is not allowed to form a government. Incidentally, the British admit that while such a coalition government was one of the suggestions, there was nothing that could be done once Mugabe received a clear majority.

A case can also be made that this was a distributive agreement. It is true that the mediator had the parties lower their resistance points. Compromise settlements that were not to the liking of either party were pushed forward, e.g., having to return to colonial rule. Deadlines were imposed and a bleak future was forecasted to whichever party withdrew from the table first. Outsiders (i.e., patrons) were constantly used to bring the parties into line, e.g., when the PF initially only offered partial acceptance of the cease-fire, the British had the Americans tell the Front-line countries that they were going to be lifting the sanctions applied to Zimbabwe-Rhodesia which resulted in the PF being pushed into an agreement by the Front-line Presidents. The British scheduled and controlled the negotiations, e.g., the PF'S answer was always asked after that of the Salisbury delegation and the parties were not allowed to engage in free debates. Carrington was aggressive in general, e.g., when Smith went up to Carrington during the negotiations and told him that these were the worst terms they had ever been offered, Carrington replied, "'Well, of course they bloody well are! You've turned down everything since the talks on [HMS] Tiger and [HMS] Fearless, and ever since the 1960s!'"(Charlton: 130).

The fate of the attempt to solve the conflict in Zimbabwe is neither explained by the intensity of the racial conflict, nor by the actors preferences about democracy, nor by their political differences. Political outcomes such as transitions to democracy are influenced by but not determined by social forces. The chance that the leaders of armed groups choose democracy increases if constitutional issues are kept separate from substantive ones. Furthermore if the path to democracy is an iterated Prisoner's Dilemma, each player must succeed in striking a balance between the need for establishing a credible threat to punish future defections from democracy and the need to alleviate the fear of defection from democracy. Third party intervention may thus aid the parties to achieve spontaneous compliance during the transition, but is no substitute for it.

However it should be noted that what started as a revolution during the liberation struggles was lost at Lancaster House in December 1979. The Lancaster House document was essentially based on West-minister-style constitution of a non-executive president with a prime minister as head of government; a bicameral legislature; an independent judiciary and an entrenched and justiciable Declaration of Rights. It also contained special protections for white minority including the provision of 20 seats reserved for voters on the white roll. The Declaration of Rights and white roll were specially entrenched in the Constitution for ten years and seven years respectively from the date of independence (Hatchard, 1991). This meant that any amendment or repeal of those provisions required the affirmative vote of all members of Parliament. Thereafter, any amendment or repeal required the affirmative votes of not less than two thirds of the total parliamentary membership. These restrictions emphasized the interim nature of the constitutional settlement and ensured that draftsmen, lawyers and academics would be busy dealing with constitutional changes for years to come. Thus the constitution could be changed to meet the interests of the ruling elites in future. However, the especially entrenched provisions precluded any immediate fundamental constitutional change. Thus, the first amendments to the Constitution between 1980 and 1987 did little to alter the basic structures. Perhaps the two most significant changes were the introduction of provincial governors and the re-organization of the Judicial Service Commission. Thus, first, the Lancaster House Constitution neither reflected the basic principles of the liberation movements nor any of their manifestos. Second, the Constitution was not a reflection of the majority African culture and value systems that the settler colonial system had brutally destroyed. The country was indeed left in the middle of nowhere.

The relatively peaceful decolonization of British and French Africa in the 1950s and 1960s led, for the most part, to the capturing of state power by a new political elite rather than a thorough-going transformation of the state structures inherited at independence. Instead of refashioning institutions in ways that might increase political participation and social justice, existing state capacities tended to <u>be marshaled</u> for exclusionary and, in many cases, authoritarian purposes.

In Zimbabwe there was no peaceful decolonization. The country was won through a protracted armed struggle. Unprecedented political changes forged in the heat of armed struggle, it is claimed, irreversibly' determined the character of the coming state' (Chabal, 1983). The imperatives of mobilizing against a recalcitrant colonialism,' for John Saul, 'inevitably involved a basic reordering of social relationships '(Saul, 1979). According to Basil Davidson, popular organization and the creation of an alternative politics meant that the new rulers would have 'no need to take over any of the structures and institutions of colonial rule' (Davidson1976). And for Patrick Cabal, 'successful people's wars usher in the establishment of states the legitimacy and structure of which owe little, if anything to their colonial predecessors (Chabal, 1983). Zimbabwe, however, did not follow this model of a state won by long and bitter armed struggle.

CRAFTING A NEW POLITICAL SYSTEM

As I have already indicated in this analysis, the battle against colonization in Zimbabwe did not run straight away along the lines of nationalism. For a very long time our nationalists devoted their energies to ending certain definite abuses, forced labor inequalities of salaries, limitation of political rights etc. It was this nationalist leadership that took over power (political) at the end of the settler colonial government, that had also agitated for independence.

CHAPTER 4

The National Independence: False Start

The victory of a seemingly militant ZANU (Zimbabwe African National Union) in Zimbabwe's 1980 independence elections, following a long guerrilla war (the Chimurenga") against White colonialism, was greeted with jubilation. Today, the hopes raised have dissipated; modern Zimbabwe (formerly Rhodesia) is marked by continuity with colonial social and economic structures.

Political, economic and social issues

The IMF and World Bank Economic Adjustment Program (ESAP) In Zimbabwe

A number of scholarly works, reviews and reports have attempted to shade light on the complex mix of factors that are responsible for Zimbabwe's current crisis of poverty. While there are sharp differences in views on the relationship between neo-liberal globalization policies and poverty in Zimbabwe, there appears to be a consensus that there is also a link between the country's agrarian issue and the government's political decisions largely taken without any economic considerations.

This review therefore does four things. First, it analyzes debates on an historical bookmark for the period of colonial economic policies in the hope that lessons from that experience will not be lost in the process of the review. Second, it reviews some of the major outcomes of pre-ESAP period economic policies. Third, it sets the stage for debate on the major issue of this review by examining the World Bank poverty paradigm of economic development. What is the World Bank strategy for poverty reduction and why has it come under severe attack from independent academics and activists worldwide? Finally, as a caution of those who will shape Zimbabwe's future, it provides some reminders of the interlocking relationships among property, poverty and conflict.

INTRODUCTION

Background to the Review

Poverty has been on the increase in Zimbabwe, particularly since the implementation of the structural adjustment program (ESAP) in 1991 leading people to blame the reforms for increased poverty. It has been difficult to pinpoint those policies, which have had an adverse effect on poverty and income distribution. This is because a wide range of policies, ranging from trade, to exchange rate to monetary to fiscal and other social policies have been implemented, often at the same time. In addition there were other exogenous shocks such as droughts during the reform period which would have contributed to poverty. Since it is difficult to pinpoint specific policies as the culprits for the growing suffering of Zimbabweans, it is difficult for policy makers to react to these increasing problems. However, there has been substantial literature praising ESAP for the economic, political and social successes the country experienced during and after the period of implementation. The literature argue that the program supported by the World Bank (WB) and the International Monetary Fund (IMF), dismantled many of the controls confining the country's economy. Implemented during a severe recession brought on by Zimbabwe's worst drought in more than a century, the program made impressive strides in trade and domestic regulatory policy, creating the basis for self-sustaining growth (World Bank Report 1998). However, opponents of this view strongly argue that the program failed to meet its goals. Poverty and unemployment increased, fiscal reforms made slow and uncertain progress, keeping the budget deficit higher than its 1989 level (Richard Saunders 1996:8).

Problems of Absolute Conclusions and the Poverty Profile.

overty has many manifestations, including lack of income and productive resources sufficient to ensure sustainable livelihoods; hunger and malnutrition, ill health, limited or lack of access to education and other basic services; increased morbidity and mortality; homelessness and inadequate housing; unsafe environments; and social discrimination and exclusion; it is also characterized by a lack of participation in decision-making and in civil, social and cultural life (World Summit for Social development 1995). Thus, it is defined and interpreted in different ways and academic debates on the subject are packed with controversies over how to differentiate the poor from the non-poor and ascertain the different levels and causes of poverty among the former. Indeed, there are also competing and complimentary conceptions of poverty and inevitably the ongoing debates are, in my view, politically and ideologically charged. I also think that constructions of poverty by researchers and policy advisors, Pvary due to disciplinary biases and ideological values. They also vary over time and space due to differences in the political, economic, cultural and ecological conditions of the contexts in question and these contexts are neither static nor closed to the outside world. It should also be noted that the distinction between absolute and relative deprivation/poverty has also been a controversial issue (Sen,1985, 1985, Townsend 1985). In the ontext of this review, globalization has become a major frame of reference for debates on poverty whether the focus is sub-national, national or international. The World Bank is actively engaged in the formation and dissemination of paradigms and interpretations of international poverty, including generally adopting a strong optimistic view of the benefits such as poverty reduction that would accrue to developing countries like Zimbabwe which have adopted its policy prescriptions for global integration. I also note that there are others who have taken more radical positions on globalization and its implications for people's well-being and cconstantly remind the world of the power structures behind the growing global inequalities (Bircham and Charlton, 2001).This overview is meant to give an idea of the diversity of perspectives in examining the real factors contributing to poverty in Zimbabwe.

Methodology and Purpose of the Review

This review undertaken here compares interdisciplinary quantitative and qualitative literature, reports, conference deliberations and public opinion in order to make an assessment of the extent to which other factors apart from ESAP, are responsible for the poverty crisis in Zimbabwe. The method used is based on comparing and contrasting different literal views to determine outcomes. The review examines historical perspectives of the impact of Zimbabwean economic policies and the origins of structural adjustment, the targets of the program and an assessment of the achievement of its goals.

DISCUSSION

Lamenting the plight of Third world countries strangled by debt, Megan Ferstenfeld (1998), work traces the origins of structural adjustment and, and why the World Bank and IMF have come to exercise so much influence over the economies of countries whose debt crisis has its roots in the larger and inherently unequal system. Historically, he documents the underpinnings of these countries' current financial disaster and traces them back to the end of World War 11, when the USA found itself in a position of great surplus relative to the rest of the world. His argument is that, not wanting to sacrifice the high levels of output it had achieved during wartime, the USA, through commercial banks, began to administer loans to developing countries in Africa, Asia and Latin America, so that these countries, I believe, could keep purchasing American goods. Ferstenfeld further notes that this North-South pattern of capital flow continued to gather momentum through the 1970s when unprecedented increases in the price of oil on the part of the nascent Organization of Petroleum Exporting Countries (OPEC) created massive profits for its members, who, in turn, inundated Northern Banks with Deposits. Thus, to properly recycle these "petrodollar" many of these banks greatly augmented their loans to developing world, resulting in virtual lending frenzy (ibid: 35).The consequences of this situation has provoked debate among economists, academicians and politicians as

Third World debt burden began to mount because of mounting interests rates caused by global recession. This meant that many donor countries were rapidly approaching the point of default, or that their accumulated debt would overtake their income from foreign aid, portending financial ruin for Northern Banks. In a desperate attempt to stop this burgeoning debt crisis the World Bank and the IMF stepped in, offering to effectively bail out the commercial banks. It was therefore in this context the concept of Structural Adjustment Lending first came into light. In my opinion, the heart of the matter is essentially that these two institutions offered to provide debtor countries with necessary loans to enable them to continue servicing their debt provided they 'adjust' their economies according to specific requirements and these requirements as Zimbabwe was to realize, soon came to be in the country's ESAP and were reflective of a concomitant neo-liberal revolution in economic thought. In my view the granting of a loan from the World Bank and the IMF implied two issues for the country. First, obtaining a loan in order to service a debt is a confirmation that Zimbabwe would be perpetually indebted. And, second, the loan has too many strings attached to the extent that the country's economic, political and social development is very much dependent on the lender. A study by Allen (1995) picked up the argument by asserting that the IMF and World Bank guidelines are not intended to benefit the implementing country but to guarantee that these two institutions could cover money loaned to Third World countries.

It has been observed that an important theoretical strand within academics and reporters on the causes of poverty in Zimbabwe revisits the colonial period to re-assess the impact of ESAP on the poverty crisis in the country. Challenging the neo-liberal view that amid the seeming success story of post-colonial Zimbabwe, there existed inherent weaknesses in the country's economy, many academics and economists are increasingly asserting the generally expressed view that the World Bank and the IMF poverty reduction program, more than any other variable, devastated the Zimbabwean economy to the extent that the incidence of poverty was immediate. (Saunders 1996) documents the manner in which the Zimbabwean government has allowed its embrace of the structural adjustment to drive many more Zimbabweans closer to the wall of poverty. Havena S. Dashwood (2000) documents the

Zimbabwe government shift from a social welfare orientation in the early 1980s to a market-based development strategy with little to no emphasis on developing rural areas or meeting the needs of the poor. She explains this shift in terms of the embourgeoisement of the ruling elite rather than the pressure from the IMF or the WB. It can therefore be argued that ESAP was not harmful to the poor; instead, the failure of the ruling elite to integrate poverty-related policies within ESAP hurt the interests of the poor. To support the argument, Dashwood analyzes both the domestic and international levels. At the domestic level, she argues, three factors led to the shift away from social welfarism: 1) an agreement among some senior decision makers that market based reforms were necessary; 2) support from entrepreneurial and agrarian elites for market reforms; and 3) the embourgeoisement of the ruling elite which refers to the acquisition of large-scale farms and big business by senior politicians and their associated desire for market reforms. At the international level, the evidence is that Zimbabwe was not in a state of crisis,(as is shown later in this review) prior to the introduction of ESAP. This indeed gave the government room to negotiate the conditions attached to ESAP. For an example the government made some attempt to protect the industrial sector during the reform period and this shows that the government had some control over the design of ESAP and could have included measures to address poverty-related concerns. In fact it was obvious that the World Bank tried to persuade a reluctant government to increase investment in social services and include a social dimensions of adjustment component within ESAP. In fact, I find this argument interesting because, I think it contributes to the debate on the African political economy literature over the relative pressure from international finance institutions versus internal domestic factors that lead to changes in economic policies. A common perception is that structural adjustment programs are forced on countries against the will of the government or the people. Thus, in my opinion, while the World Bank did exert some pressure, the impetus for reform in the case of Zimbabwe came from changes in the domestic class structure.

However, work by Saunders (1998), Ziumbe (1999), Sichone (2003) and Machemedze (2004) contradicts Dashwood's argument by contending that in 1990, the Zimbabwe government succumbed to Western donor pressure and grudgingly agreed to implement the five year economic structural adjustment program, as a response to the economic crisis which had been afflicting the country since independence in 1980. Collaborating this argument, Kanji's(1991) work reveals that some adjustment measures had already been introduced but the adoption by the Zimbabwe government of ESAP marked the beginning of a new, more intensified phase of structural adjustment. Thus the argument presented here, in my view, is that Zimbabwe asked for WB and IMF intervention in order to transform the country's tightly controlled economic system (a legacy of a sanction-inflicted economy of the colonial regime), to a more open, market-driven economy. In fact, my observations are that there were a number of factors that had held back growth and participation by the poor. A study by Chimanikire (1991-92) also links poverty to the country's history. His argument is that the pre-independence conditions tended to bestow economic and political benefits on whites as opposed to blacks. It is true that the African population was settled on poor quality and small portions of land whilst whites occupied vast tracts of fertile land. Blacks were also denied equal education and employment opportunities and even salaries for the same job differed with race. These policies introduced great inequalities and also perpetuated poverty among the African population. Works by Nyathi T, and Makoni, K.,(2000) notes that the prolonged liberation struggle which led to independence in 1980, had adverse effects on the entire African population and the resulting economic hardships were felt most severely in the rural areas. Loewen son, and Chisvo (1997) also observed that the imposition of sanctions on the then Rhodesian regime affected the entire country particularly the African urban and rural poor. Thus, my argument here is that colonialism had a determining influence on Zimbabwe's economic condition. While it is increasingly implausible to attribute the country's economic ills to colonialism, the neglects of that period—in the development of the physical and human capital stocks, technological capabilities, and institutions—made it predictable that the new state would have great difficulties in sustaining reasonable rates of economic progress, just as it is not surprising that the colonial experience, and the way this interacted with traditional social structures, resulted in a post-independent Zimbabwean state that would often prove incapable of responding adequately to emerging economic deficiencies.

But what of the contemporary influence of the world economy as represented by international institutions? In taking up this set of issues, Rukobo's (1997) study examines the methods the new Zimbabwean government adopted in dealing with the economic imbalances of the pre-independent era. At independence, one of the major challenges for the new state was that of redressing the inequalities of the past, as already mentioned above. Rukobo notes that this was done through the adoption of welfares policies, influenced by socialist convictions of the Zimbabwe African National Union-Patriotic Front (ZANU-PF) government. With growth with equity, as a major objective, accent was placed on education, health, rehabilitation of the war raged infrastructure, removing discriminatory laws and promoting the advancement of women (Chitiga-Mabugu 2001), and the resettlement of the landless people. Studies by Chisvo and Munro (1994) examined agricultural production as the other major area of policy emphasis. The work reveals that agricultural production led to sustained agricultural production by the peasant and small scale sector. It would therefore seem to me that the first 10 years of independence witnessed remarkable progress in redressing social imbalances, and laid a foundation for a sound human resources development policy. Nevertheless, it should be noted that, the economic policy operated on a regime of controls and regulations, which was exacerbated by the monopolistic nature of the economy. Development and growth by 1990, were thus sluggish, unemployment levels rose, and balance of payments problems became intractable. Climatic factors, particularly drought, added a thorn in the flesh, especially in 1992.

The Zimbabwe government Central Statistical Office (July 1998: 1-2) shows how imbalance between central government expenditure and revenue compromised the sustainability of the spending program. The Central Statistics reveals that central government expenditure as a share of the national economy was always high and international standards, and revenue fell short of expenditure through the 1980s. It further notes that at independence, central government expenditure accounted for about 35% of GDP, and partially due to the social sector investment of the 1980s, this share rose 47.4% by 1988/89. The gap between expenditure and revenue and interest payment on the national debt began to consume greater share of the government budget. Budget deficits also crowded out private investment and created inflationary pressures. In my view, though the policies of the 1980s seemed conducive to sustained economic growth, the Zimbabwean economy began to stagnate in the mid to late 1980s. This is evidenced by Government's recognition of the need for a strong economy that could provide resources necessary to combat poverty and redress the imbalances of the past. As a result of the deteriorating economic growth, high inflation rates, high levels of unemployment, and increasing fiscal budget deficits, Zimbabwean authorities fell under pressure to abandon the interventionist policies of the early 1980s in pursuit of market-oriented reforms.

The evidence surveyed would support Zimbabwe's move to economic reform. My argument is that when the country embarked on its economic structural adjustment program (ESAP) in 1991, the decision came from the recognition that main constraints to growth were the low levels of investment, and the administrative management of the economy inherited from the Unilateral Declaration of Independence (UDI) period, reinforced by the socialist experiment of the 1980s. In the context of this review, it is significant to note that the Zimbabwe government approached the World Bank, the IMF and other donors for financial support for ESAP. Indeed the support was forthcoming, although it was conditional on the implementation required. Indeed, Zimbabwe today faces political and economic crises as a result of multifaceted chain of events emanating from ESAP, which was introduced by the IMF and the World Bank (WB). But to say the IMF and the WB are solely responsible for these crises, in my opinion, would be a misrepresentation of facts but their policies have played a huge part in triggering the problems the country is facing. Allen (1999) and Machemedze (2004) h studies on the agreements and implementation of ESAP show that when Zimbabwe started implementing ESAP, a number of sectors of the economy were affected and this led to ordinary people suffering the consequences. The studies also note that in implementing the structural adjustment program, the government adopted the so-called Washington Consensus (WC) principles, which in effect reversed the otherwise steady growth of the economy that the country was experiencing. This view of course is refuted in the studies by Chitiga (2004) and White et al.(2001) who are of the view that there were other exogenous shocks such as droughts during the reform period which could have contributed to poverty. However, Allen and Machemedze note that the IMF and WB principles included:

1. Fiscal and monetary policy reforms, including budgetary and monetary stabilization measures, and the liberalization and deregulation of banking and finance.

2. Trade liberalization, including the abolition of quantitative controls and the reduction and harmonization of tariffs and duties.

3. Deregulation of wages, interest rates and exchange rates.

4. Public sector restructuring, entailing the downsizing of the civil service and the reorganization and commercialization of parastatals.

5. A social safety net in the form of Social Dimensions Fund (SDF) for those vulnerable to the adverse effects of structural adjustment.

Critics of the IMF and the WB in Zimbabwe claimed that these guidelines principles and guidelines were intended not to benefit the implementing country but to guarantee that these two institutions could recover money loaned to Third World by the Northern Banks. It was therefore not surprising that in the midst of implementing some of these principles, the government encountered multiple problems from different fronts, including from its own people, labor unions, the private sector, civil society, from multilateral and bilateral donors, including the IMF and the WB. Donors squeezed the country to enforce further changes to the economy that was rather protected from foreign manipulation before the 1990s Machemedze (ibid:1). It was this situation which, in mid-1990, made Zimbabwe agree with the WB to implement a home-grown five year phased program towards a free market. J.Alwang (1990) study shows how during the first year, Zimbabwe was to lift many restrictions on imports, meaning drastically reducing tariffs on products coming into the country. The study also reveals that at the donor's conference in Paris

March 1991, the WB and western countries promised US$690 million to fund the first year of the program. He shows how the donors backtracked, demanding more rapid changes than originally agreed.

In my own interpretation these rapid changes that the donors wanted entailed free fall financial, capital and trade liberalization. The free fall liberalization exposed the country to foreign products and control thus mortgaging the nation to the dictates of foreign commercial interests at the expense of their social and moral well-being.

According to the WB, the reforms under ESAP could hardly be regarded a roaring success. They did not lead to a marked improvement in investment and savings levels as a percent of the national income. The economy became much more outward oriented, and exports increased substantially. Private sector profitability grew principally in agriculture, tourism and transport, and the informal sector had a strong boost. However, fiscal and monetary stability remained elusive and the standard of living declined for many, particularly urban households, with percentage of households classified as poor rising from 40% in 1991 to over 60% in 1995. Unemployment continued its relentless `rise. Little progress was made in land reform. The considerable achievements in health and education made during the first decade after independence also came under threat, with the brunt of the fall in public expenditure being borne by the social sector. Dhliwayo (2001) details a study on the impact of public expenditure management on basic social services. In fact his study assesses the situation of basic services in particular health and education under ESAP examine the impact on various sectors of the population, particularly low-income groups children and the poor from the resulting changes in social welfare. His concludes that according to civil society, the removal of subsidies and cost recovery in education and health sectors has resulted in swelling numbers of children out of school, people dying of curable diseases in their homes and women giving birth at home or in scotch carts on their to health centers. Civil society also contends that several health indicators have deteriorated. Participation in parental services have declined; maternal death and mortality rates of babies born before arrival have increased, etc.,

Also, studies by (Sachikonye, 1997; Kanyenze, 1999; Loewen son, 1999) extensively examine the effects of ESAP on various other aspects of the national economic activities. The studies draw the following conclusions:

a) ---The average of employment growth during ESAP period was half the growth of the labor force, meaning that the new jobs were not being created fast enough to absorb new entrants into the labor market. In any case as I have pointed out earlier in this review, by focusing exclusively on the urban formal sector as the engine of growth, the program neglected the sectors with greatest potential for job creation, i.e., the informal and small, medium-sized enterprises

b) ---With reduction, or in some cases elimination of subsidies private companies were forced to reduce costs in order to remain competitive. Deregulation allowed them to make increased use of temporary, part-time contract workers who did not receive benefits and had no job security. These changes increased unemployment and decreased real wages. As a matter of fact, those who found full time jobs were no longer guaranteed a living wage, and the effects of these reduced incomes had been made even more impotent by rising prices. The collapse of wages meant that workers live below poverty line.

c) ---The failure to modernize technologically also devastated local industries hit by cheap imports, as well as by the loss of government subsidies, high interest rates, and the increased cost of raw materials. Small and medium-sized industries were forced to reduce production, go out business or switch from manufacturing to importing, leading to a large drop in manufacturing input. With companies forced to lay of workers, employment dropped sharply between 1991 and 1998, accompanied by a serious erosion of wages and salaries.

d) In the agricultural sector, note should be taken that at the time of ESAP, the country met all its domestic food needs and still had enough maize and wheat to export to other countries in the region. With the advent of structural adjustment, trade barriers, price controls, subsidies and price quotas were removed. Farmers were no longer required to produce food for local consumption. In fact, some commercial farmers shifted from maize growing to even producing flowers for the international market.

e) The studies further show that with budget allocations for rural infrastructure in rural areas down, farmers lacked good roads and adequate transport systems, as well as processing, storage, and distribution systems, they required in order to be competitive. Other key problems faced by farmers under ESAP, include lack of access to land, difficult with availability and price of farm inputs, the loss of important and timely information previously provided by the marketing boards.

CONCLUSION

Economic policy during colonial and post-colonial Zimbabwe has not resulted in improved socio-economic welfare of the populace. Consequently, economic decline has resulted in widespread political discontent and disaffection with the present regime. As political tensions have reached a political impasse, there are concerns that Zimbabwe's economy is on the brink of collapse primarily because of the IMF and WB – sponsored ESAP, and, in my opinion, because both the government and markets have failed the poor. In fact most institutions in the country still have colonial structures not capable of responding to new socioeconomic and cultural demands. Central government institutions still emphasize control and are sector ally structured. To ensure continued human development and poverty reduction, the country needs to provide adequate resources and targeting on activities most in need of public support---and to devise burden-sharing mechanisms that will ensure that the poor have access to basic social services.

Reducing poverty will require growth in employment and increased productivity in smallholder agriculture. These in turn will be dependent on economic growth, continued investment in human capital, and an increase in the assets owned or controlled by the poor, including land. Also, while sound macro management and an improved incentive framework will help to put the economy on a stronger growth path, public expenditure will need to enhance participation, provide supportive infrastructure, and protect those whom the benefits of growth do not reach.

Chapter 5

Restoration of Legacy: Neo-colonialism

In the past 7 months Zimbabweans have witnessed a hive of activity in terms of efforts to revive Zimbabwe's economy. In the advent of the military power takeover, which saw the ouster of Robert Mugabe and the forceful ushering in, of Emmerson Mnangagwa, as head of state, there has been hyper activity under the "Zimbabwe is open for business" rhetoric. However there has been little indication (if at all), that there is any improvement on the ground.

This author seeks to analyze the direction our politicians have taken, in their quest to revive the economy, which desperately needs resuscitation.

The country has witnessed the President making, in excess of 15 sojourns, to countries across the world, with bowl in hand, scarf in neck, begging investors to come to Zimbabwe with their money. The China trip saw deals worth billions of dollars being signed, (dozens were signed before by Mugabe to no avail). Included in the deals as the country was told, were the supply of buses worth in excess of $500 million, for urban commuting. In excess of $1 billion worth of clothing in the form of ZANU PF regalia was also sourced from China on the same trip.

But are we desperate to find investors, so much as to waste the resources available, in travel expenses on the taxpayer's account? Is this money not better used for other purposes, to alleviate the dire situation in our country?

What is the purpose of posting ambassadors to foreign countries if they cannot seal deals for the country? This article will interrogate this strategy by the President and his government in detail.

The country has also witnessed the opposition leaders make several trips, to the US, UK and South Africa, to engage(as they say), foreign governments and potential investors, in preparation for when/if they win elections and takeover government. We have even witnessed them telling (lying to) voters about how Trump promised a $15 billion windfall, should they win the election, and how they will build a $100 billion economy within a few years, sprawling with bullet trains and airports at growth points. Pensioners have been promised compensation of their lost pensions, while depositors who lost their savings in the RBZ's Gideon Gono era, were promised US$ pegged reimbursements. We have also witnessed the so called opposition economists, together with their president, vowing that they will end the cash crisis in 14 days of winning elections. They have promised a cash injection from somewhere outside the country. What country would splash cash in such a way without due diligence and collateral security in return? A sudden return of confidence in the banking sector, is also being pledged, and the cash crisis will just vanish overnight and banks will start dishing out cash at ATMs, simply on the basis of the opposition being in charge. They also believe that all those hoarding money in their homes will suddenly take it into the banking system.

This article will also interrogate these opposition pronouncements, so as to test their feasibility and reliability.

Is lack of foreign direct investment (FDI) the cause of the downfall of Zimbabwe's economy? Is FDI the real and most important means of reviving Zimbabwe's economy?

It is imperative that we interrogate this seemingly important model of economic revival.

As stated above, the idea of lack of FDI as the main obstacle to Zimbabwe's revitalization has been permeated by both government and the opposition. But it is not the means to the revival of the economy. Zimbabwe is not even hungry for FDI as both the ruling party and the main opposition alliance would like the people of Zimbabwe to believe.

This article will explain why FDI is only secondary to what is required.

RESTORATION OF THE ROTTEN GOVERNANCE CULTURE

Before any attempt to revive Zimbabwe's economy begins, whoever is or will be in charge of the country after 1 August 2018 must start by analyzing and reversing the rotten governance culture that has slowly but steadily ingrained itself into the country's governance system.

Zimbabwe over all the years of its self-governance, has developed a culture of institutionalized corruption, nepotism, theft and plunder with impunity, protection of criminals and general disregard of the law. This culture has infectiously entrenched itself in government, quasi government institutions, local authorities, in the private sector and in society in general. Government departments like the Registrar General's office, which encompasses the issuing of passports, birth certificates, identity cards and death certificates, is well known for its corrupt activities. Other departments like IMMIGRATION and ZIMRA, have not been spared by this virus.

Jobs have been given on the basis of cronyism, family ties and sexual favors. Competency, transparency and accountability have been thrown out through the window.

Parastatals and other quasi government institutions have not been spared. Those in charge of these departments and institutions have plundered the resources belonging to the organizations they lead with impunity and gracious approval from the politicians in charge. The politicians have encouraged this, as they became the major beneficiaries of the plunder by civil servants, whom they appointed through nepotism and cronyism.

Tenders for government and quasi government projects are now given to briefcase cronies. A point in issue is the recent granting of the tender for Presidential travel arrangements being granted to the wife of the coup leader, turned Vice President, with neither following tender procedure nor provision of requisite documents by the potential contractor.

The November power take over, which tis author has always called a coup, brought in a so called New Dispensation, which came with the slogan, "Zimbabwe is open for Business". The New President started with a trip to the Davos World Economic Forum, where he started telling the world that the country was now open for FDI. This he did before he had done anything on the ground to change the country's way of doing business.

But is it really open for business? Who had closed it in the first place? The answer to this is simple. When Mnangagwa took over the government with the help of the military, he appointed most members of the former Cabinet into the same positions they had previously occupied, and shifted a few into new portfolios.

When the military took over, they stated that they were hunting for criminals around then President Mugabe. But no one has ever been arrested and or charged with any crime, nor brought before the courts, to date. The nation was told that those who externalized money would be shamed, as well as arrested if they didn't return the money within a specified amnesty period. Nothing was ever said about that, nor was anyone brought to book or shamed.

The same corrupt system is in charge of government, including the already corrupt civil service, and no attempt has been made to cleanse it. It is the very same system that closed Zimbabwe for business. How then would we expect to have a cleaner, newer, more efficient administration with the same corrupted system in place? The same corrupt elite has siphoned cash out of banks, government institutions and companies they control. They have vast loads of cash in their houses and abroad, while the country is on its knees. Some of their children have been arrested at borders trying to smuggle the cash out of the country, whether it was for business transactions or offshore banking, but no court proceedings against them have successfully been concluded. The VP challenges the populace to use plastic money for all transactions, yet he is seen counting US$100 notes in public.

It is therefore futile to waste time soliciting for FDI when the same porous system is still intact.

CLEANSING THE ROT IN THE BANKING SECTOR

Reserve Bank currency leakages which result in money turning up on the streets and at borders, instead of banks, is a menace that needs to be reversed before any solution is sought to Zimbabwe's crisis. Whether it is the RBZ itself or the commercial banks, responsible for this, the President needed to have resolved this crisis before jumping onto the plane to foreign lands.

It is clear that this rotten system involves syndicates which are controlled by high ranking politicians. The country has heard of companies associated with the President's sons controlling the movement of cash from the RBZ, into the black market.

Control of key sectors of the economy by the likes of John Bredenkamp, Billy Rautenbach, and Nicholas van Hoogstraten, who are well known for allegations of underhand dealings and uncouth influence on governance, in partnership with the ruling elite, makes it difficult for sanity to ever prevail. Van Hoogstraten, who has convictions in the UK is allegedly influential in ZANU PF circles and has funded the party's activities in return for protection of his property empire. Bredenkamp is known (according to Wikipedia)for sprucing up the Smith regime in the UDI era and involvement with the current political elite in the arms trade during the DRC war.

Rautenbach on the other hand is a specified person in South Africa for tax evasion and or other cases. He has been involved in mining in the DRC and was once put on sanctions over his alleged involvement in the DRC war, which he denies. Apart from his family transport business empire, he is involved in the Green Fuel project in Zimbabwe, which involves senior ZANU PF politicians.

The three are alleged to have corruptly built empires in the mining, agricultural, oil, wildlife, manufacturing. and transport sectors, in connivance with politicians.

Their murky involvement and influence in Zimbabwe's economy with politicians, retards the current regime's clean slate on good governance.

Even if billions of dollars are brought in through the RBZ for disbursement to banks and onto customers, it will end up on the streets and back outside the country. Drastic measures will need to be implemented if any sanity is to prevail in the country.

The system has had a perpetuated, dysfunctional, despicable, and illegal culture which is not easy to turn around, if the people in charge are still the very people who presided over the growth of the culture. It is a tall order for this or any incoming government to achieve, let alone within the timeframe so peddled by the main opposition.

The commercial banks themselves have not been spared by the corrupt culture, as they have jumped onto the bandwagon of hoarding and dishing out cash to their directors, their family members, preferred associates and customers for so called burning. Depositors' money is dished out to friends, relatives and politicians as non-performing loans, ahead of the productive sector. The loans are spent on lavish parties, luxury holidays, expensive cars, boyfriends and girlfriends. The productive sector of the economy has been left wallowing in financial dire straits while banks divert the money. Some of the banks have ended up under curatorship, with depositors losing their savings.

Bankers have also leaped onto a culture of quick-buck harvesting by charging exorbitant bank charges, which fleece customers of their hard earned cash. Mobile money transfer companies have joined the band of greedy entities and fleece customers of their money by charging unscrupulous fees.

While President John Magufuli of Tanzania, at his inauguration, banned foreign travel by government officials, including himself, and instructed that all foreign business being handled by relevant High Commissioners and Ambassadors in the foreign countries, President Mnangagwa travels across the globe, with delegations in excess of 50 at a time, all reaping hefty packages in per diem allowances at the expense of the fiscus. The Presidential delegation, instead of using the national airline, charters expensive private aircraft. The Tanzanian Vice President, on the few trips abroad, has used the national airline, in economy class, with ordinary citizens. Where Air Tanzania does not ply, he connects on ordinary commercial airlines that ply those routes, with a skeletal delegation, to save taxpayers' money.

THE PRIVATE SECTOR

The private sector is also complicit as they are also engaged in the quick-buck syndrome and all corporate governance has been thrown into the bin. Profits are no longer considered in the standard 15 to 25 percentage mark, but in the 100 to 200 percent earnings.

Buyers in the private sector have become the richest employees, by conniving with cronies and brief case businessmen to fleece companies of money by awarding inflated purchase orders, which has destroyed profitability of enterprises.

So there is no sane sector of the economy which can embrace or sustain any realistic change of culture under the current governance system. Until and unless the top echelons start cleansing themselves of the culture they created and maintained, it is futile to invite any foreign investors for meaningful revitalization of the economy. Only illicit money launderers, drug peddlers and illegal arms dealers would happily jump on the opportunity, while countries that regard their own interests ahead of the Zimbabwe's well-being, would rejoice. A case in point is the UK, which is seeking its own opportunities, after exiting the European Union. The UK does not care about good governance in Zimbabwe as long as it's trade interests are achieved, and its glory and dominance is reinstated over its former colony.

The opposition also talks of solving the cash crisis in 14 days of taking power. They talk of getting a windfall from some foreign funder, who will pour billions into the banking system. Unless and until the corrupt and financially immoral culture is rooted out first, the cash crisis will not recede overnight.

Confidence with a new government alone is not enough to bring back money into the banking sector, as the opposition economists believe. As long as the syndicate that controls the illicit and porous system is still intact, it is futile to pour in money into the sector. Cleansing of the whole sector is necessary and cannot happen in 14 days, without shaking and destabilizing the country's economy. Reinventing or creating a new governance culture will take more than one term of a Presidency at least.

REVIVAL AND SUPPORT FOR THE PRODUCTIVE SECTOR

As mentioned earlier in this article, the President was quick to travel abroad to try and lure investors. While it may be good to bring in investors, it is ingenuous to focus on foreign investors, while ignoring local business. Zimbabwe has always had enough investment in all essential sectors. It is the corrupt culture that has scared away and or stifled both local and foreign businesses.

Zimbabwe is still mining gold, platinum, nickel, diamonds, coal, emerald, granite, and many other minerals. All these minerals are exported, but where are the proceeds going? Who is getting the foreign currency?

The country has already been over mortgaged to foreign countries like China against natural resources, and further mortgaging will deprive future generations of their inheritance. Government must refrain from seeking loans and or grants pegged against the country's resources as has been happening. It must seek trade and investment with emphasis on local beneficiation, like the establishment of smelting plants for platinum and cutting and polishing of diamonds locally.

The manufacturing sector has been left to disappear into oblivion, rendering the whole nation jobless, while the country is now a net consumer, flooded with inferior Chinese products and South African GMO produced foodstuffs.

If government had the slight sense of national empathy, it would have started by looking inwards, to the local productive sector, and find ways to stimulate productivity and create employment. Foreign currency that is being earned from mineral exports would be directed at assisting the productive sector import raw materials for production to create employment.

Manufacturing and exporting businesses used to hold nostrum accounts, with banks, where they would keep their foreign currency for purposes of importing raw materials, machinery, tools and equipment. These were raided by the RBZ when it desperately needed foreign currency to fund its misplaced priorities. This was another reason business stopped banking foreign currency with banks. So, for government to restore confidence in the business sector, it has to restore these nostrum accounts and devise a robust policy preferably legislation, which must prohibit the Central Bank from raiding such private accounts. This will instill confidence in business and they will feel safe to deposit their money in banks.

The Chinese and other Asian owned businesses are well known for keeping their cash away from banks, including foreign currency. This they do with collusion from high ranking officials who even help them smuggle it out of the country. The arrest of four people of Asian origin recently, allegedly with US$4 million in cash and 100 kgs of gold is a stark example of this menace. Any serious government must uproot this scourge before talking of Zimbabwe being open for business.

The author mentioned earlier that the President went to China to seal so called deals, among them, the deal to purchase in excess of US$500 million worth of urban commuting buses. The import of chief's vehicles was also misplaced. ZANU PF used foreign currency to import campaign vehicles and party regalia.

If that money had been allocated to W. Dahmer, WMMI, and Quest/ Leyland to import kits for those buses and vehicles to be locally assembled, it would have gone a long way in promoting local industry and creating much needed employment. This author has always viewed Themba Mliswa as one maverick who is an opportunist, and a former beneficiary of the rotten system, but I must commend him for his fight in Parliament, when he demanded that vehicles for MPs be assembled by WMMI instead of being imported. Although this was ignored, it was a noble suggestion for the good of the economy.

It may be argued that the buses and vehicles were a donation from China, or that China had given a condition that the loans or grant was to purchase only Chinese goods. However, the government must be able to set its parameters so that it will not be squeezed into compromises by these so called donor partners.

Zimbabweans have noticed that all contracts given to the Chinese, utilize almost 100% Chinese raw materials and equipment, including laborer's. It is ironic that government allows that even locally available materials and equipment are replaced by those from China. Zimbabweans wallow in poverty for lack of jobs while China exports its labor into our country, and wherever locals are employed, they're abused by these foreigners.

Government must not accept contracts drawn under such conditions.

Many important industries which closed because of government policies, could easily revive, if the corruption running through society is uprooted. Companies such as Dunlop Zimbabwe, Kariba Batteries, and others were solid and sustainable industries which were destroyed by a corrupt governance system. Zisco Steel was Africa's renowned steel supplier, but is lying idle, while the country is left to import steel products from South Africa and China.

In the first days of this new government, there was hype and fun fare, with promises Zisco would be opened in a few weeks. Nothing has happened 7 months down the line. Bickering and demands for shares in the company or cuts by politicians has been reported as the obstacle to its revival.

There was pomp and fanfare when refurbished Transnet locomotives were imported and commissioned by the President. But they failed to take off, as they derailed one after the other. This clearly shows lack of both vision and organizational intelligence. The NRZ railway tracks need rehabilitation before we even think of buying new locomotives. The NRZ radio communication system is dilapidated and needs absolute reconstruction, but we rush to import useless and incompatible locomotives.

The textile industry has seen, companies like Merlin, National Blankets, David Whitehead, Julie White and others being neglected by government, opting to import party regalia from China. Zimbabwe, a country formerly endowed with its own cotton industry, has been reduced to a net importer of textiles and clothing. Second hand clothing has been allowed to be smuggled through Mozambique in bales, destined for Mupedzanhamo and other flea markets. The cotton industry has been relegated to oblivion yet the country was well known for quality cotton and textile products. Bata, Conte Shoes and G&D shoes, which supplies shoes across Africa have been left to sink into oblivion.

The new government is shouting "Zimbabwe is open for business ", while it fails to ensure the revival and protection of its own industries.

The construction industry in Zimbabwe was second only to South Africa, with both solid technical expertise and industrial base, enough to meet the needs of any infrastructural development. The country has a wide pool of engineers who are doing wonders in developing other countries across the world. Zimbabwean engineers are well known in organizations like Network Rail in the UK for developing sustainable transport systems. But our government is calling for foreigners to come and perform shoddy infrastructural development, while neglecting its own human resource base.

While the politicians fly each other to foreign lands for treatment, the ordinary citizen dies in local hospitals for lack of medicine. The White City bombing incident clearly showed the reality of the leadership's attitude. They flew each other to South Africa for treatment while the aides and others were left to wallow at Mpilo where some eventually died.

Zimbabwe had pharmaceutical companies that manufactured most of the country's medical equipment and drugs, such as CAPS Holdings, but they're now history. Government, instead of working on reviving such industries, they spend money on foreign medical trips for themselves.

Reviving such industries like CAPS should be government's priority instead of these "Zimbabwe is open for business" slogans without support of local industries.

SIGNING OF THE AFRICA TRADE AGREEMENT

As the author mentioned earlier about the President signing the Africa Trade Agreement in Kigali, it is good to be seen signing such agreements on regional and international protocols. But is it beneficial to Zimbabwe at this juncture?

Zimbabwe does not have any products that it currently exports, save for mineral raw materials, which are not for the African market anyway. So what will Zimbabwe benefit at this juncture from this agreement? Products from other countries across Africa will land in Zimbabwe tariff free, which will in effect stifle the growth of local industries.

My opinion is that Zimbabwe should have ensured the growth and protection of its manufacturing and export industries before signing such an agreement. Any such agreement should have been signed after extensive consultations with all stakeholders such as manufacturers and heads of industry bodies.

Nigeria and South Africa, the two largest economies in Africa, refrained from signing, citing their need to consult their countries' stakeholders. They would both benefit more from this agreement than all other countries, but did not sign, because they consider their local stakeholders more than international partners.

If Zimbabwe had such an attitude towards its local business, it would not have hastily signed the agreement, before ensuring its local industry is ready for that.

The President also attended the commissioning of the Kazungula rail road bridge, which actually bypasses Zimbabwe. Although Zimbabwe was said to have been eventually been made a partner, it is hardly beneficial to the country, as all traffic will bypass Zimbabwe, and will be a loss of revenue for the country.

THE CHINESE EXPERIENCE

When China moved from its communist path, towards economic development, Deng Xiaoping, created a very articulate formula to develop China's economy. Deng never visited foreign countries, nor did he meet foreign leaders to seal deals on FDI. He concentrated on ensuring that the internal laws and mechanisms in his country were conducive both for local business and foreign investors. The adage that goes, "charity begins at home" was one of Deng's main tools. Deng crafted policies that began to pluck out corruption, and enable local business to thrive.

He ensured the protection of local industry by demanding that any foreign company that invested in the country's special economic zones, must employ local labor, wherever there was no expertise that required foreigners. He ensured that the investors implement technology transfer and use local raw materials wherever they were available.

Deng promoted partnerships between foreign companies and Chinese state enterprises, which have now developed into fully fledged multinational companies. An example is ZTE, whose major shareholders are the China Aerospace Science & Industry Corporation and the China Aerospace Science and Technology Corporation. China's FDI policy demanded total transfer of technology to the local workers, and it bore fruit. Today Chinese state enterprises, whose shareholding is now diluted by local private shareholders, are world leaders in technology. They remain attached to the state through part ownership and through towing national policy.

Contrastingly, Zimbabwe's model of FDI policy is haphazard and confusing. State enterprises like the ZMDC have partnered foreign diamond mining companies, but remain broke and mismanaged. One cannot tell where the revenue from the mining is going. The local state enterprises do not have a grip on the daily management of the mining and are oblivious of the quantity, quality or value of the diamonds mined and exported.

CONCLUSION

Change itself is a daunting, time consuming and arduous task. It is challenging enough to change one's personal habits, let alone entire institutions or government. Attraction to the status quo and cognitive dissonance hinder significant change.

Nevertheless, that's what must be demanded by the President and the government, with zero tolerance to any form of criminal behavior in any sector of both government and the general economy, private sector included. But it has not been forthcoming. The current government is so entangled in this corrupt governance system, and benefits from it, that even if FDI was to be poured into the fiscus, the leakages the author mentioned earlier will devour it all and leave the economy in the same state.

In conclusion, it is this author's firm belief, that Zimbabwe needs to cleanse itself of the toxic governance system that has reduced it to a pariah state. Government then needs to invest more on assisting local businesses to revive themselves and protect them against foreign domination, if Zimbabwe is to ever develop itself back to its past glory and surpass. Zimbabweans must develop their own country.

References

Bayer, Resat. 2002: Lord Carrington's Mediation of the Rhodesian Settlement:

Zimbabwe's Second Chimurenga Concludes: Journal of Peace and Conflict Resolution 1.4

REFERENCES

Allen, T.W. Structural Adjustment in Zimbabwe: The World Bank Perspective; Harare, September 2, 1999, pp. 3-4. Awang, J. "Changes in Poverty in Zimbabwe Between 1990 and Awang, G. T, 1996:" Development in Southern Africa, Vol. 18, N December 2001, Routledge, Taylor and Francis, 2001

Amartya Sen, Oxford Economic Papers 1985: 37: 659-668

Baluch, Bob, and Ursula Grant, "Poverty Inequality and Growth in Sub-Saharan Africa, (quoted in African Poverty at the Millennium: Causes, Complexities, and Challenges 2001.

Charlton, Michael. 1990: The Last Colony in Africa: Diplomacy and the Independence of Rhodesia. Oxford: Basil Blackwell.

Chimanikire D.P. Zimbabwe and trade Liberalization, Peace Review, Winter 1991-92 California, pp. 49-51

Chitiga, M-Mabugu, L. Income Distribution Effects of Trade Liberalization: A CGE Analysis" in C. Mumbengegwi (ed.) Macroeconomic and Structural Adjustment Policies in Zimbabwe 2001

Chisvo, M. and Munro, L. A Review of the Social Dimensions of Adjustment: UNICEF, Harare, 1994

Chitiga, M. Report submitted to poverty and economic policy (PEP) research network (first version still unedited) 2004
Central Statistics Office(SCO), Government of Zimbabwe, Harare, July 1998, pp. 1-2

Bowman, Larry, W. 1973. Politics in Rhodesia: White Power in an African State: Harvard University Press, Cambridge, Massachusetts

Davidow, J. 1984: A Peace in Southern Africa: The Lancaster House Conference on Rhodesia 1979. Boulder: Westview.

Dashwood, Hamena. Zimbabwe: The Political Economy of Transformation: Changes in Structure and Development in Zimbabwe During the Period from 1980-1997; Toronto: University of Toronto Press. 2000, ppxii 252

Dhliwayo, R. The Impact of Public Expenditure Management Under ESAP on Basic Social Services: Health and Education: SAPRI/ Zimbabwe 2001

Habeeb, William, M. 1988 Power and Tactics in International Negotiations: How Weak Nations Bargain with Strong Nations: Baltimore: John Hopkins University Press

Loewen son, Randy Chisvo, M. (1997) "Rapid Transformation Despite Economic Transformation and Slow Growth: the Experience of Zimbabwe, in S. Mehrotra and R Jolly (eds) Development with a Human Face: Experiences in Social Achievement and Economic Growth, Clarendon Press; Oxford, 1997.

Loewe son, R. "2001 Budget : Enough to Make You Sick, Daily News, 21 November 2000

Kanyenze, G. "The Implication of Globalization on the Zimbabwe Economy: Paper Prepared for the Poverty Reduction Forum, Harare,1999

Machemedze, R. Zimbabwe and the IMF—Time for shifting from neo-liberal paradigm to people centered development alternative: Zimbabwe and the IMF-SEATIN-2004

Nyhamar, Tore. 1980. Transition To Democratic Constitutions In Ethnic Conflicts.
http//www.gmu.edu/academic/nyhamar.html

Nyathi,T. and Makoni, K. ESAP and Ordinary People, SAPRI, 2000

Stedman, S.J. 1991 Peacemaking in Civil War: International Mediation in

Zimbabwe, 1974-1980: Boulder: Lynne Reiner Publishers.

Stedman, S.J. 1993. "The end of the Zimbabwean Civil War." In R.Licklieder, (ed.) Stopping the Killing: How Civil Wars end. New York University Press, pp.125-163.

Tamarkin, M. 1990. The Making of Zimbabwe: Decolonization in Regional and International Politics. London: Frank Cass. Walter, Barbara F. 1997. The Critical Barrier to Civil War Settlement: International Organization, Vol. 51. No. 3.(Summer,1997), pp.335-364. Watkins, M; Rose grant, S.2001. Breakthrough International Negotiation: How Great Negotiators Transform The World's Toughest Post-Cold War Conflicts.

Ferstenfeld, Meagan. Structural Adjustment: Time for Reform: Third World Countries Strangled by Debt: in Houston Catholic Worker 11/12/98

. Rukobo, A.M. Structural Adjustment and Poverty Alleviation Strategies in Zimbabwe: Institute of Development Economics, (IED) Tokyo, 1997

Sachikonye, L. Report on Assessment of the Impact of Land Reform Program on Commercial Farm Worker Livelihoods, Farm Community Trust of Zimbabwe, May 2002

. Saunders, Richard, Economic Structural Adjustment Program (ESAP) Fables11, Southern Africa Report, SAR, Vol.11, No. 4, July 1996, p8 "Zimbabwe".

. Sen, A.K. A Sociological Approach to the Measurement of Poverty—A reply to Professor Peter Townsend, Oxford Economic Papers 1985: 37: 669-676

Townsend, P.A Sociological Approach to the Measurement of Poverty –A rejoinder to Professor

. Ziumbe, F. Africa View, Work on a Sustainable Society: A view from Africa, 1999

Zartman, I. W. 1989. Ripe for Resolution: Conflict and Intervention in Africa. Oxford: Oxford University Press: (ed.) 1993. The Unfinished Agenda: Negotiating Internal Conflicts. In Stopping the killing: How Civil Wars End, Edited by Roy Licklider. New York: New York University Press.